Twelve Sunday Mornings with Pastor John Hagee

A SERMON DIGEST

Volume 2

First printing, January 1994
ISBN 156908-015-1

© 1992 and 1993 by John Hagee and Global Evangelism Television, Inc. No part of this book may be used or reproduced in any manner whatsoever without written permission, except in the case of brief quotations embodied in critical articles and reviews. For additional information write John Hagee Ministries, P.O. Box 1400, San Antonio, TX 78295-1400.

Books by Pastor John Hagee

9 Bible Principles for Judging Prophecy

101 Facts About Satanism In America

Being Happy In An Unhappy World

Bible Positions on Political Issues

Communication in Marriage

Should Christians Support Israel?

The Miracle Of Grace

The Power To Heal

Twelve Sunday Mornings with Pastor John Hagee

Volume 1

Volume 3

Twelve Sunday Mornings with Pastor John Hagee

Contents

Seven Secrets of Success

1. Your Attitude Toward Success 7
2. Qualifying For Success 23
3. Investing For Success 36
4. Success Without Stress 46
5. Success Through Excellence 59
6. Success Through Perseverance . 69
7. Success That Loves 82

Blessing or Curses

8. Curses: Their Cause and Cure 95
9. America Under Curse 109
10. The Blessing: Power & Purpose 122
11. Defeating Depression 136
12. You Can't Go Home Again 149

Seven Secrets of Success

Chapter 1
Your Attitude Toward Success

All of us want to be successful, yet so few of us are. According to the Social Security Administration, only 2% of Americans reach the age of 65 financially independent. Of the remainder, 30% depend on charity, 45% depend on their relatives, and 23% have to work the rest of their lives.

It is God's desire for every one of you to succeed. The Bible says, "Beloved I wish above all things that thou mayest prosper and be in health, even as thy soul prospereth" (3 John 2). "Even as your soul prospers." That phrase means that the spiritual realm controls prosperity in the natural realm.

Prosperity and success begin in your thought life, in your decisions. You decide to accept or reject Christ in your mind. You decide which emotions will rule your life. You decide to accept defeat or to climb the unclimbable mountain. You decide to feel inferior or to say, "I can do all things through Christ." That's a decision process. The Bible says, "As [a man] thinketh in

his heart, so is he" (Proverbs 23:7).
Success is not accidental. It is a by-product of your attitude, and your attitude determines your attainment. Your attitude toward God determines the eternal destiny of your soul. Your attitude toward people will determine whether you are a friend or a foe. Your attitude toward wealth determines whether you will ever have it — and if you get it, whether it will destroy you or make you happier.

Success is not accidental

It is God's will for you to prosper. But you must hear God's word and obey it before success can be yours. That's what our text says today:

> *This book of the law shall not depart out of thy mouth; but thou shalt meditate therein day and night, that thou mayest observe to do according to all that is written therein: for then thou shalt make thy way prosperous, and then thou shalt have good success.* (Joshua 1:8)

Success is not accidental; it is a by-product of your attitude. Has anyone ever told you that you have a bad attitude? People fling that phrase around today like salt and pepper. "You've got a bad attitude." So what does that mean? It means you're too critical. It means you're too sarcastic ... too arrogant ... too mean ... and too inflexible.

If you have a bad attitude, it means that you generally choose to disagree. You whine and pout when you can't get your way. You like to live with a chip on your shoulder. You can't keep friends. You can't keep a job. You can't keep a wife or a husband, because you are a joyless toad. You're like Leona Helmsley, Donald Trump, John McEnroe, and Attila the Hun all rolled into one. Who is responsible for your attitude? You are. We try to blame our attitude on our husband or wife. We blame our attitude on the weather, the car we're driving. We blame our attitude on the IRS or PMS — we blame it on something, anything, except ourselves.

But you choose your attitude every morning when you get out of bed. David said, "This is the day which the Lord hath made; we will rejoice and be glad in it" (Psalm 118:24). Your attitude is a choice, not a chance. Do you wake up in the morning saying, "Good morning, Lord!" or "Good Lord, it's morning!" There's a difference in those two.

Do you feel like if you inherited General Motors somebody would outlaw cars? Is someone always raining on your parade? Do you feel like the only way you can wake up in the morning with a smile on your face is to go to bed at night with a coat hanger in your mouth? You've got a bad attitude.

Two men looked out through prison bars; one saw mud, the other saw stars. Two men in the same situation, but two opposite reactions.

A Tennessee newspaper carried the story of two young men who had been jilted during their engagement. They made a choice about their attitude. One chose to jump off a bridge and commit suicide. The other decided to write one of those "somebody done somebody wrong" country songs. And he got $75,000 in royalties.

How do you change a negative attitude? You get a new attitude not from the New Age, but from the New Testament. Paul writes, "Whatsoever things are true, whatsoever things are honest, whatsoever things are just, whatsoever things are pure, whatsoever things are lovely, whatsoever things are of good report; if there be any virtue, and if there be any praise, think on these things" (Phil. 4:8).

Do you get mad thinking of something that happened in your past that still angers you? Paul said if you will think about things that are true, honest, just, pure and lovely — put that kind of thinking into practice, he says, "and the God of peace shall be with you." (Phil. 4:9).

If you think about the right kind of things, you'll have the right kind of attitude and enjoy the peace of God. But if you read trash and hang around with bums, pretty soon you'll be a trashy bum. "As he thinketh in his heart, so is he" (Prov. 23:7).

Quit worrying about what happened to you in the past. All of us have had something to hurt us in the past. God is a healer of broken hearts. He puts dreams back together again. Forget the past and "press toward the mark for the prize of the high calling of God in Christ Jesus" (Phil. 3:14).

Quit wading around in the bone yard of your miserable past and stand in the winner's circle with Jesus Christ. Quit whining about your circumstances. Quit blaming your mother or father, or God or the government — or everyone on planet earth — for your failures and mistakes. You are a child of God. You were born to win. Get up off your face, dust yourself off and get back in the race. You can be victorious through Christ the Lord.

The Bible: your success manual

Are you searching for success? Then read the Bible, Mr. Businessman. This book is better than the Wall Street Journal and the Forbes 500. This book predicts market trends hundreds of years in advance: it's called prophecy. This book tells you eight things that will kill every business venture. (Stay tuned, that's coming in part two.) This book tells you who not to go into business with. This book tells you how to have an ROI that will produce a 10,000% return. An ROI is "return on investment." Who wouldn't like to have a 10,000% return on an investment?

Listen to the financial advice of Joshua. "This book of the Law" (that's God's word), "shall not depart out of your mouth" (that's your speech), "but you shall meditate therein day and night" (that's your thoughts), "that you may observe to do all that is written therein" (that's obedience), and then afterwards — after you speak the word, after you think the word, after you obey the word — "then thou shalt have good success."

That's a guarantee — not from Prudential, not from the Metropolitan Life Insurance Company — but from God himself. That's a guarantee worth living by. "Then thou shalt have good success."

The definition of success

What is success? If you can't define it, how will you know when you've found it? If you're going nowhere, any road will take you there. Success is progressively, systematically moving toward your God-given goal in life. If you have no goal, you will never succeed. How would you like to watch a football game that had no goal? The guy who got the ball would just start running all over everywhere. That describes your life if you have no goal. Success is not making lots of money. If the only reason you're living is to make a lot of money, you're living for a very shallow reason. Money can buy you a $50 steak, but only God can give you the appetite to enjoy it. As for me, I can eat anything that will slow down. But I've had lunch with millionaires who had Maalox in one hand and crackers in the other. They're afraid somebody's going to get their money. I guarantee you, somebody will. When you die, they'll strip you naked and dress you in a suit with the back cut out. They'll bury you in a box and all your money is going to be gone, forever out of your reach.

Money can buy you the finest surgeons, but God can give you the health to never need them. Money can buy you a bed of absolute, pure gold, but only God can give you the peace of mind that gives you true rest. Money can buy you a mansion, but only the love of God will make it a home.

What is your definition of success? To a drug addict, it's another fix. To a politician it's getting re-elected. To the average American, success is the gratification of the instinctual man: to get what I want, when I want it. But you cannot satisfy the instinctual man. The instinctual man is driven by greed. He is driven by the world, the flesh and the devil. The only thing that will satisfy your soul is Jesus Christ.

For me, success is to preach the gospel of Jesus Christ in this city, to America, and to the uttermost ends of the earth by every means I can. I am systematically progressing toward the goal of seeing tens of thousands born into the kingdom of God. Evangelism is what my life is about, winning lost people to Jesus Christ.

For a Christian, success is serving the Lord with all of your heart, soul, mind and body. It is a seven-day-a-week experience. Success does not mean being accepted by the world. Every week I get letters saying, "Preacher, if you could just tone it down a little bit, maybe that group over there would accept us." Let me tell you something. I don't want that group over there to accept me, I want God to accept me. Jesus said the world hated him and it would hate me. The Bible says light does not have fellowship with darkness. James said that a friend of the world is the enemy of God. If your idea of being successful is that everybody speaks well of you, hear the word of God: "Beware when all men shall speak well of you!" (Luke 6:26). There's something wrong with you when everybody speaks well of you.

God wants you to succeed

The Bible, the law of God Almighty, gives clear guidelines concerning success. These are the basics. First, it is God's will for you to succeed. Moses wrote in Deuteronomy 8:18, "But thou shalt remember the Lord thy God: for it is he that giveth thee power to get wealth." Power to get wealth does not come from your genius, it comes from God's goodness. You don't have the power to take your next breath, even as you pound your chest and congratulate yourself for being a self-made man. You ought to deny it, to save yourself the liability.

Psalm 1 says, "Blessed is the man that walketh not in the counsel of the ungodly ... But his delight is in the law of the Lord; and in his law doth he meditate" (think) "day and night. And he shall be like a tree planted by the rivers of water" (unlimited resources), "... and whatsoever he doeth shall prosper" (verses 1-3). After you think upon and act upon God's word, you are destined to prosper!

Some of you read the word of God, you think about the word of God, you speak the word of God, but you don't act upon it. You don't obey the word of God. Nothing good is going to happen until you act.

When Jesus came to the pool and saw the man who had been crippled for 38 years, he told him, "I want you to act upon what I am saying. Take up your bed and walk." That man could have looked at Jesus and said, "Hey, you're an itinerant carpenter who just walked up on the scene. I've been by this swimming hole for years and nothing good has ever happened to me." But he didn't say that. He immediately obeyed the Lord and got up, and instantly he was healed.

Your attitude determines your attainment. A good attitude will produce a good result. A bad attitude will produce a bad result, every time.

Are you a Paul or a Thomas?

Consider the examples of St. Paul and Doubting Thomas. St. Paul said, "I can do all things through Christ which strengtheneth me" (Phil. 4:13). Paul was beaten three times with 39 stripes. (By Roman law you could only whip a man 39 times, because anything more than that would kill him.) Paul was stoned and left for dead. He was shipwrecked. Although innocent, he was thrown into prison. He was cursed, he was kicked, he was spit upon. How many of you know that would hurt your self-esteem?

After he was stoned, Paul did not climb on his pity pot and roll out his lower lip to whine and complain about suffering for Jesus. He never developed a negative attitude. He picked his bloody body up out of the dirt and went back into the city where he had almost been stoned to death, and he said, "Hey, about that sermon I didn't finish preaching — here it is!"

Paul wrote the book on True Grit, not Rooster Cogburn. Paul said, "We are troubled on every side, yet not distressed; we are perplexed, but not in despair; persecuted, but not forsaken; cast down, but not destroyed" (2 Cor. 4:8-9). Paul would not quit and he could not be defeated. Paul wrote that we are more than conquerors through Jesus Christ (Romans 8:37) and we can do all things through Christ who strengthens us (Phil. 4:13).

Compare that with Doubting Thomas. He had been with Jesus for three years. He had seen the sack lunch that fed 5,000. He saw Lazarus walk out of his grave. He saw the funeral parade that became the resurrection of a widow's son. He had seen all of those miracles. But at the first negative thing, when the first hurtful thing came down the road, Thomas mounted his self-piteous throne. And whining and whimpering down the streets of Jerusalem he said, "I knew we'd get in trouble if Jesus kept preaching those sermons about the government." The disciples came and said, "Thomas, Jesus is alive." And he said, "Oh, I can't believe that. I'm just too hurt. Not until I see it on CNN or Dan Rather tells me it's true. Not unless I can touch the scars in his hands."

Everybody has been hurt at some point in their life. There is something all of us could go back to and wail about if we chose to. In Jesus' name, grow up and get over it! Look to the future. Forget those things that are in your past and say, "With God's grace, tomorrow is going to be a better day."

Which one of these people are you like: Doubting Thomas, whining and self-pitying, or the apostle Paul, undefeated and undiscouraged? Which one of those two are you like? It's your choice. Your attitude determines your attainments.

What's your excuse?

Here are excuses people use. They say, "Oh, I can't do that." I *can't* do that is the brother of I *won't* do that. Life does not consist of what you want to do, it consists of what you ought to do.

People say, "Oh, I'm too old." Moses was 80 years old when he became the pastor of six million people. When you're 80, you're just getting started. Grandma Moses started painting when she was 80. Some of her paintings sold for a million dollars. I can hardly wait until I get to be 80. I'm going to get a Weed Eater and dip it in five gallons of paint and throw it all over a canvas and frame it and sell it!

Then people say, "I'm not smart enough." How smart is that? I've graduated from three universities, and some of the dumbest people I ever met are in those schools. Believe me, I am pro-education. But I also know that you can get a degree without getting an education. It happens all the time.

Some people say, "I can't do that. I'm handicapped." How handicapped is that? Helen Keller, who was blind and deaf, graduated from college with honors, wrote books and became a well-known speaker. My children have heard me say that so many times they hate Helen

Keller. Report card day at our house is known as Helen Keller Day.
You attitude is not determined by your handicaps or your circumstances. It does no good to say, "If my circumstances would change, I would change." Wrong. If you'll change, it doesn't make any difference what your circumstances are. You choose your attitude, and your attitude determines your success.
Look at the circumstances of Jesus' life. He was born a member of a hated minority. Are you a member of hated minority? You can get bitter, or you can get better. Jesus didn't allow that to whip him. His birth was considered illegitimate. He lived in scandal every moment of his life. Rome said he was a traitor. The religious leaders said he was a heretic. He was crucified between two thieves and buried in a borrowed grave. When he came out of the grave, he didn't go to his disciples and say, "Run for your lives I never dreamed it would be like this."
Jesus, the night before Calvary, told his disciples, "These things I have spoken unto you, that in me ye might have peace. In the world ye shall have tribulation: but be of good cheer; I have overcome the world" (John 16:33). He did not say that from ivory-towered walls of security. He said it the night before he was to be slaughtered as the Lamb of God on Mt. Calvary.
I am here to tell you today that God is greater than your circumstances ... God is greater than your heartache ... God is greater than the divorce you've just gone through ... God is greater than the bankruptcy you've just endured ... God is greater than any crisis you're facing. Lift up your heads and rejoice, the living God is within you! You are more than a conqueror!

Change your attitude, not your circumstances

When Paul and Silas were beaten again and thrown in jail at Philippi, they could have thrown up their hands and been defeated by their circumstances. Paul could have said, "You know, Si, when I was ordained as the chief Pharisee in the National Council of Churches, I was appreciated. I had a horse allowance. I was on national television with all the biggies. Whenever I came on stage somebody said, "Heeeeeeere's Paul!" I was sharing my testimony all over the nation, how I was killing all those Bible-believing, right-wing fundamentalists. Then God mugged me on the road to Damascus, and ever since then I've been beaten and stoned. Nobody loves me any more. Do you think God really wants me to live this way?"

That conversation never happened. The Bible says they sang in the midnight hour in jail. While the blood was dripping off their backs, while the rats were circling them, while their hands and feet were locked in the stocks, they began to sing, "All hail the power of Jesus' name, let angels prostrate fall. Bring forth the royal diadem and crown Him lord of all!" You don't think they sang that? I do, and this is my sermon, so that's what they sang.

As God heard that two-man concert, he rose from his throne and looked over the balconies of heaven. He reached down and put his fingernail in the soil beside that jail and vibrated the earth until that jailhouse exploded and the prison doors fell off their hinges. Paul and Silas walked out with the jailhouse keys in one hand and a convert in the other. Why? Because they did not let the circumstance control them, they controlled the circumstance with an attitude of faith, not fear.

If you'll have faith and not fear ... if you'll start praising instead of pouting ... if you'll start acting like a victor instead of a victim, great things will start happening in your life today.

You've got to succeed somewhere, so start where you are with what you have. Bloom where you're planted. "Well, I don't have anything," you say. With God, that's enough. I went to the university on a football scholarship and I was poorer than Job's turkey. One day I was talking to a student whose father owned the King Ranch. I bragged to him that I had something money couldn't buy. He looked at me and said, "And what would that be?" I said, "Poverty." Change your attitude even if you can't change your circumstances.

There are all kinds of religious excuses people give to hide behind their failure. "Jesus was poor, and I want to be like him." Jesus described his kingdom as a place where they use gold for asphalt, where the gates are of solid pearl, and where mansions designed by the architect of the ages have foundations of diamonds, rubies and sapphires. If that's poverty, I want to try it.

What about the verse that says, "The foxes have holes, and the birds of the air have nests; but the Son of man hath not where to lay his head" (Matt. 8:20)? Here's the explanation for that. The foxes refer to Idumean Jews, half-breed Jews, like Herod. Jesus said of Herod, "Go tell that fox" (Luke 13:32). Get the connection — fox. The "foxes" are the Idumean Jews. The "birds" are the Romans. Everywhere you turned your eyes there was an eagle, the symbol of Rome. They put an eagle on the temple in Jerusalem and it caused a riot among the Jews.

What Jesus was saying is, "These foxes, these Idumean Jews that persecute us like Herod, they have a place, and the Roman soldiers have a place. I am the son of God, I created this place, yet I have no place on this earth, because I don't want a place here. My kingdom is not of this world, it's is in your heart. My kingdom is a greater kingdom and you're a part of that kingdom. Don't look at what Rome is trying to do, don't look at what Herod is trying to do, look at the treasure that I have. It's greater than anything you've ever seen before. Trust me and live for me and you'll rule and reign with me." That's what Jesus was saying.

What about the verse that says you can't serve God and mammon (Matt. 6:24)? The key word is *serve*. You can't serve money and serve God. But you can be a friend of God and be plenty wealthy. Abraham is called the friend of God and he was an exceedingly wealthy man. Solomon had gold hinges in his horse stable — that's better than Ross Perot! I know people driving a 20-year-old car held together with baling wire who love money and can't get their hands on it. They're broke, but they're still serving money.

Acting on God's word

Listen to the positive speech in the word of God —

"My God shall supply all your need according to his riches in glory by Christ Jesus" (Phil. 4:29). Notice it says "need," not "greed."

"Beloved, I wish above all things that thou mayest prosper and be in health, even as thy soul prospereth" (3 John 2). Remember the connection between spiritual prosperity and success.

"The young lions do lack, and suffer hunger: but they that seek the Lord shall not want any good thing"

(Psalm 34:10).

"The Lord is my shepherd; I shall not want" (Psalm 23:1).

"And all these blessings shall come on thee, and overtake thee, if thou shalt hearken unto the voice of the Lord thy God" (Deut. 28:2). The Lord will give you cities you didn't build, wells you didn't dig and vineyards you didn't plant (Deut. 6:10-11). If you will honor God, he will give you the power to get wealth. He desires that you prosper until the wicked look at you and say, "Why are they prospering?" And the wicked shall say, "They are the children of the Lord and the blessing of God is upon them." That's God's will for your life!

But as you think the word and speak the word, you have to act on the word of God. Here is where so many Christians stop — they won't act on the word. Moses had to put his rod in the water before the sea would divide. Peter had to get out of the boat before he could walk on the water. Elijah had to pour water on the sacrifice before the fire fell from heaven. Do you think he understood that? No, he did not.

If all that you ever obey is what you understand, then you'll never obey God. Some of you will only follow the Lord as far as your logic can understand what God is trying to do — which means you'll never get to the first grade in faith. The man with the withered hand had lots of logical reasons why he shouldn't even try to stretch it out. But in obedience to the word of God, he did it.

Many of you want to succeed, but your thought life is poisoned with anger. You're filled with bitterness and resentment over the past. You want to succeed, but you have no goal, you have no defined purpose. Perhaps you're trying to succeed without God, patting yourself on the back as a self-made man. You've waited for your circumstances to change rather than your changing your attitude. You've lived in self-pity, making religious-sounding excuses, when God is saying, "If you'll put your hand in my hand, I'll make you greater than anything you ever dreamed of being."

Chapter 2
Qualifying for Success

We are constantly being required to qualify in every area of our lives.

Have you ever gone to the bank for a loan? If you enjoy going to the bank for a loan, you probably enjoy root canals and IRS audits. A banker will ask you a series of obnoxious questions like, "Do you have a job? Is there the slightest chance you'll ever be able to pay this back?" If you don't qualify for the loan, out the door you go.

When you apply for admission to a university, you must qualify. The admissions board will want to know your GPA. They'll look at documents like report cards, and ask unpleasant questions like, "Did you attend class? Did you pass any subjects other than bubble blowing and lunch?" If you didn't, you're not going to get in that university. You don't qualify.

Every doctor, every lawyer, every accountant, every teacher has to qualify before being approved by a state board to practice a trade. And thank God for that. When I'm lying on a gurney and a doctor comes at me with a knife in his hand, I want to be sure he knows the difference between an appendectomy and a hysterectomy.

God is no different. Every thing God offers in his word, you must qualify to get it.

In theology it is called a propositional revelation. Do you want salvation? If you will confess your sins and believe in your heart that Jesus has been raised from the dead, God will forgive you of your sins. If you do not confess your sins, your sins will not be forgiven. Do you want to be saved? Joining a church will not save you. Do you want to be saved? Giving to the poor will not help you. Perhaps you say, "Well, I'm going to be saved because God loves me." No, that's not right. God loves everybody, but you are saved only when you confess your sins and receive Jesus Christ as Lord. If you haven't done that, you don't qualify. You're lost.

"Well, I'm sort of saved." You can't be any more "sort of saved" than you can sort of shoot a shotgun. You either are or you're not. If you've never received Jesus Christ, if you've never confessed him as Lord and Savior, then you're lost and without God. You may be moral, you may be a good person, but you're eternally lost.

Do you want healing? If you can believe, all things are possible to you. Without faith it is impossible to please God. People who say, "I don't believe in miracles" won't ever get one. You will believe when you need one, but you won't ever get one until you start exercising your faith.

Do you want to prosper? Here's how to qualify. "Give, and it shall be given unto you;" how? "Good measure, pressed down, and shaken together, and running over" (Luke 6:38).

Everything that God controls, gives. The sun gives the light of day. Plants give food. God the Father loved the world so much that he gave his only begotten son. Jesus Christ gave his life a ransom for many. If you have a problem with giving, you are not God's child. If you have a problem with giving, you are not controlled of the Holy Spirit, because everything God controls, gives. "The Lord loveth a cheerful giver" (2 Cor. 9:7), but he will take from a grouch.

8 things that disqualify you for success

Here are eight things the Bible says will disqualify you from ever having success. These eight things will kill every business deal, and God will guarantee you poverty if you practice just one of them.

1) *Idolatry.* Idolatry is defined as the worship of a physical object as a god, or immoderate devotion or attachment to something. Most Christians would say, "Pastor Hagee, this is America; very few people are into idolatry here." That's wrong. I would dare say the majority of this audience are involved in some kind of idolatry. The first commandment says, "Thou shalt have no other gods before me" (Exod. 20:3). Not rock stars, not movie stars, not athletic stars; just the Bright and the Morning Star, Jesus Christ.

I'm talking about idolatry, the inordinate devotion to anything other than God. How much time do you spend watching *As the World Turns, General Hospital, Rin Tin Tin* or CNN? Who gets prime time in your life? Compare the time you watch the tube to the time you spend reading God's word. Who or what is the lord of your life? Who has the influence over your life, Hollywood or the Holy Spirit? That's a legitimate question.

Consider the god of intellectualism. 1 Samuel 15:23

says, "for rebellion is as the sin of witchcraft, and stubbornness is as iniquity and idolatry." Who is stubborn? The man or woman who will not change his/her opinion even when the word of God says he/she is wrong. Their opinion has become their god. When you refuse to hear the word of God and stubbornly stick with your unbiblical opinion, you are in intellectual idolatry.

We wouldn't dare think of allowing someone to join the church with a statue of Buddha around his neck. But this church and every church in America is filled with stubborn, stiff-necked people. And God says, "When you read my word and will not obey it, I will cut you off because you are an idolator." So idolatry is the first thing that will cut you off from God's prosperity.

2) *Laziness*. If there's a great book on the work ethic in the world, it's the Bible. The Bible says, "Six days shalt thou labor, and do all thy work" (Exod. 20:9). God worked, and some of you ought to try it. It would be a new experience for you. 1 Timothy 5:8 says that he who does not provide for his own family has denied the faith and is worse than an infidel (unbeliever).

Nothing in your life is going to work until you do. Work hard: the job you save may be your own. Many people are fascinated by work. They can sit down beside it and watch it for hours. One boss was asked, "How many people work here?" He replied, "About half of them."

Americans have been led to believe we ought to get more money for doing less work. That's socialism, and socialism leads to poverty. Get excited about your job. There's a word for people who aren't excited about working, and that word is unemployed. Successful people make themselves do what they hate to do. A failure will wait until his boss makes him do it. Which one of those groups are you in?

If you're a Christian, you ought to be the best worker in your company. When your boss gets ready to lay people off, he wouldn't dare think of letting you go because he can't do without you. If you're a Christian doing a sleazy job, your boss ought to fire you tomorrow, because you ought to be working circles around everybody else.

3) *Waste*. Proverbs 18:9 says, "He also that is slothful (lazy) in his work is a brother to him that is a great waster." How much money, how much food, how much time do you waste? The average American throws enough food out the back door every day to feed a family of 5 in another part of the world. Jesus fed 5,000 out of one boy's sack lunch and then he commanded the disciples to pick up the leftovers. Why? Because waste is wrong. Waste leads to poverty.

Do you waste time? To waste your time is to waste your life. You have 168 hours per week. You can't get more, and you don't have less. You can't put time in a bank, and you can't stop it. The Bible says to redeem your time (Eph. 5:16). Squeeze the juice out of every minute and you'll have an exciting life.

4) *Borrowing*. I'm talking about things that bring poverty according to the word of God. Proverbs 22:7 says that the borrower is servant to the lender. Every bank you borrow from makes you a slave. Every credit card you have in your pocket makes you a slave. One of the quickest ways to financial success is plastic surgery — cut up your credit cards! This morning I'm looking at a house full of slaves dressed in silk. When you come to understand debt like the Bible sees it, you'll see it as a cancer.

5) *Stealing*. Theft brings poverty. Zechariah 5:3

says, "This is the curse that goeth forth over the face of the whole earth: for every one that stealeth shall be cut off," and that means financially. God says if you're a thief, he'll bless you with poverty. Do you steal from your employer? Do you steal on your expense account? Do you borrow things permanently? You're a thief, and God says he will cut you off.

We saw in Los Angeles, under the excuse of social injustice, people going into stores and stealing one thing after another. Right there beside every name that stole even one thing, God wrote "poverty" beside their name. The government can pour 50 billion dollars into Los Angeles and it will not get out of hock, because of the sin of theft.

6) *Crooked deals.* The sixth thing that will cause poverty is the crooked business deals of the father. Proverbs 17:13 says that if a man pays back evil for good, evil will never leave his house. If a father returns evil for good, evil will follow his children all the days of their lives.

In American history there are several prominent businessmen whose children inherited great wealth, but the tycoon's children lived under a curse of tragedy and sorrow. Why? Because the fathers built their fortune on crooked business deals. They drove people to financial ruin and stepped on the poor, and God sent a curse to that family. The only way the curse will be removed is for restitution to be made four-fold. That's God's formula for restitution.

7) *Anti-semitism.* An anti-Semite is someone who hates the Jewish people because they're Jewish. You will never succeed as an anti-Semite. You don't have to agree with the Jewish people. You don't have to let them run over you in a business deal. But if you hate them

because they are Jewish, if you hate them because they're wealthy, if you hate them because of their brilliance, God will cut you off.

God told Abraham, "I will bless them that bless you, and curse him that curseth thee: and in thee shall all families of the earth be blessed" (Gen. 12:3). That is still God's foreign policy statement concerning the Jewish people around the world.

Jesus said in John, the fourth chapter, that salvation is of the Jews (verse 22). Abraham, Isaac and Jacob were Jews. All of the prophets of the Old Testament were Jewish — Jeremiah, Isaiah, Ezekiel, Daniel — not a Baptist in the bunch. And then come Mary, Joseph and Jesus, all Jewish people. The disciples, Jewish people. St. Paul, Jewish. It's not possible to be a Christian and not love the Jewish people for their contribution to Christianity. We wouldn't be here without their contribution.

8) *Refusing to tithe.* The eighth thing that will disqualify you for success is the refusal to tithe. Why should you tithe? Because tithing is God's financial plan for world evangelism and your personal success. Tithing is what the church did before bingo, and I'll say more about that in a minute.

These eight things will disqualify you from success. When you participate in any of these things, God just reaches over and turns your tap off. You can work as hard as you want to, but you're not going to get ahead; you're not even going to catch up.

Why you must qualify for success

Why must you qualify with God? Because "the earth is the Lord's, and the fullness thereof" (Psalm 24:1). The "fullness" includes you and every body else on the planet. It is the Lord who gives you power to get wealth (Deut. 8:18). "The silver is mine, and the gold is mine, saith the Lord of hosts" (Haggai 2:8).

Have you heard of the golden rule? Those who have the gold make the rules. God says, "It's all mine. You meet my rules and obey my rules for success, and I will bless you with a blessing you can not contain. If you refuse to obey my rules, get used to poverty, because you'll have it the rest of your life. It's your choice."

God controls the wealth of the world for the benefit of his children. He has power over the sun, the moon and stars ... over presidents and prime ministers ... over General Motors, Ford and Chrysler ... over your job ... over your mother-in-law. That's real power!

This is the God whose power performance begins in Genesis and does not stop until the book of Revelation. This is the God that divided the Red Sea for Moses and then covered the chariots of Egypt with the same water. The bloated corpse of Pharaoh floated to shore with his signet ring, the symbol of his power, still dangling on his rotting hand. "Who is the Lord that I should obey him?" That's what Pharaoh had said. In the waters of the Red Sea he found out just how powerful God really is.

God rained manna six days a week for 40 years for Israel. He was the cloud by day and the fire by night. He held the sun still for Joshua. He was the fourth man in the fire with the three Hebrew children. They wouldn't bend, they wouldn't bow and they wouldn't burn. He rained fire from heaven for Elijah. He turned water into wine at the feast of Cana. He healed every disease and cast out demons with a word.

All of this power controls the wealth of this world for God's children. Psalm 112 says that wealth and riches will be in the house of the man who fears God and delights in his commandments. Wealth and riches — God controls that. Proverbs 13:22 says that the wealth of the wicked is laid up for the just. Think about that. How would you like for the wealth of God to be poured into your business, to be poured into your finances, to be poured into your health? Would you like God to pour out a blessing on you you couldn't possibly contain? The sad truth is, most of you don't qualify.

God wants you to have his abundance, but he cannot let you have it until you start obeying him. And if you have a problem with giving, you can give up ever having God's abundance.

How to qualify with God

Here is how to qualify for success. The first step is to become God's child. Why? Because God owns it all and he controls it all for the benefit of his children. Are you qualified to pray, "Our Father which art in heaven, hallowed be thy name"? Not until you've received God the Father through Jesus Christ. Jesus said, "I am the way, the truth, and the life: no man cometh unto the Father, but by me" (John 14:6). These days people are running around saying there are lots of ways to be saved. No, there's not. There's just one way, through Jesus Christ the Lord.

Is God your father? Jesus told the Pharisees they were of their father the devil (John 8:44). Jesus taught the disciples to pray, "Our Father which art in heaven." So there are two fathers and there are two families. To which family do you belong? David said, "I have been young, and now am old; yet have I not seen the righteous forsaken, nor his seed begging bread" (Psalm 37:25). Believe me, the unrighteous are forsaken every day. If you really want to prosper, plug into God the Father through Jesus Christ. Start obeying his word and good things will happen to you.

Why are so many people in India starving to death? Because they have rejected God as their father and God has no responsibility to take care of them. Their gods are cows and they feed those sacred cows grain while babies are starving to death in the streets. Rats eat more precious grain and spread disease, but they don't kill the rats because they might be one of their reincarnated relatives. While the people starve to death, the cows get fat and the rats prosper.

Step two in qualifying for success is to learn the joy of giving. I repeat, everything that God controls, gives. And when it comes to giving, some of you stop at nothing. (You'll catch that in a minute.)

The Bible says, "Give, and it shall be given unto you." Why does God require giving to qualify you for success? Because receiving without giving destroys you. When you receive without giving, you become miserly and stagnant and dead. The Dead Sea is dead because all it knows how to do is receive. It takes in, takes in, takes in, and gives nothing out. There is no outlet, and so the waters accumulate and stagnate. There is not one live fish in that sea. It is a testimonial that death comes to people when all they do is receive.

Our government, through welfare, gives people something without expecting something back. That produces beggars, not bread winners. The motivation to work dies. They become parasites, not producers. Every able-bodied person in America needs to get off welfare and go to work, NOW! And if you don't have the courage to do it, the government ought to cut you off.

Receiving without giving destroys you. If you want to destroy your child, give them everything they want without expecting anything back. He'll be absolutely worthless by the time he's 18. God's law says when you receive, give something back.

When you go to Dillard's and pick up a shirt, you give them $20. It's a T-shirt, but you give them $20 anyway. When you go to Albertson's and pick up your groceries, you give them something in exchange. When you come to the house of the Lord, when you are saved and healed, when you experience the love, joy and peace of the Holy Spirit, God intends for you to support his kingdom. God gave his son for your redemption, what have you given to Him?

How much should a Christian give? Malachi 3:10 says, "Bring ye all the tithes into the storehouse." The tithe is 10% of what you make, the storehouse is the church. God says the result will be this: "I will open the windows of heaven and pour out a blessing on you that you're not able to contain." Would you like prosperity to run over you like a Mack truck? Tithe 10%.

"Preacher, do you really expect me to give 10% of my income to God?" No, I don't; but God does. I'm in Sales, he's in Management. What does he manage? Your breath, your heartbeat, trivia like that. You want to tick him off, go ahead.

Tithing is God's plan for financial success

Why tithe? Because it's God's financial plan for you. The money you spend for lunch today will last about four hours. Money spent for a car will last 36 months, maybe. (Notice how they self-destruct when you send that last payment to the bank?) But money spent for the kingdom of God will last forever. The Bible says to lay up for yourselves treasures in heaven. The day is going to come when all that you will have is what you've given to God.

Why should I tithe? Because God commands it. The Bible says to bring all the tithes into the storehouse. Not "if you feel led." He says do it. Do you pay the IRS because you feel led? No, you do it because it's the law.

Why should I tithe? Because God calls those who don't tithe robbers. Malachi 3:8 says, "Will a man rob God? Yet ye have robbed me. But ye say, wherein have we robbed thee? In tithes and offerings."

If you don't tithe, God sees you as a crook. He's got your picture on his "most wanted" bulletin board in heaven. Some of you came to church this morning wearing stolen clothes and stolen jewelry, riding in stolen cars. You took God's tithes and offerings and bought those things. And God's computer in heaven has a red light flashing beside your name. Beep, beep, beep, poverty, poverty, poverty.

If you don't believe that, read the ninth verse of Malachi 3. "Ye are cursed with a curse: for ye have robbed me." I didn't write that, God did. If you don't give, you are living under a curse. You will work harder and make less. You will financially struggle regardless of your income. Whatever you make, it will not be enough. Why? Because you're in rebellion to the will of God.

You say, "Look, I know a guy who never tithes and

he's rolling in money." No you don't. You know a guy who's storing it up so he can go to the Methodist hospital where a surgeon will split him open like a field-dressed deer and get all his money in one day.

The people who prosper long-term are the people who obey God's word and who qualify for success according to his principles.

Chapter 3

Investing for Success

The Bible is the greatest investment manual ever printed. The greatest business principles in print are in this book I hold in my hands. And what you're going to learn today will turn your life upside down and guarantee you wealth without risk, if you have faith enough to practice what's written in God's word.

Jesus said, "Lay not up for yourselves treasures upon earth, where moth and rust doth corrupt, and where thieves break through and steal: But lay up for yourselves treasures in heaven, where neither moth nor rust doth corrupt, and where thieves do not break through nor steal: For where your treasure is, there will your heart be also" (Matt. 6:19-21).

Investments are exciting. Jesus knew that. As he was preaching one day, to arrest the attention of his audience, Jesus said, "My kingdom is like a treasure hidden in a field" (Matt. 13:44).

Now, suppose I told you that last night I went to the vacant lot next to the church and buried a treasure chest filled with millions of dollars. How many of you would get up and go look for it? There would be an instant vacuum in this church. You'd rip the doors off at the hinges and dash out in your silk suits and high heels to dig for the hidden treasure. The Bible is the treasure map, written by the King of the Ages, and if you will obey it, you will be blessed in this life, and in the life to come, beyond your wildest dreams.

Jesus wanted every one of his children to become master investors. Out of 38 parables, 16 of them deal with how to manage your possessions. That makes how to handle your investments one of the most important issues in the Bible. Scripture says more about how to manage wealth than about heaven and hell combined. There are more than 2,000 verses on financial prosperity and how to handle your material possessions.

Jesus taught us that investing is a must. The man who does not invest has no future. Jesus gave us the parable of the talents in Matthew 25. A talent was a sum of money, equal to roughly $5,000. To one man the master gave five talents, to another two talents, and to another one talent. The man with five talents invested them and doubled his money. The man with two talents did the same thing. But the man with only one talent buried it for safekeeping. When the master of the house returned, he commended the servants who had invested the money wisely. When he came to the man who had buried his one talent, he rebuked the servant and gave the one talent to the servant who had turned the five talents into ten.

The message is this: what you don't invest, you lose. If you mismanage God's resources, he will take it away from you and give it to somebody who will invest it in the kingdom of God. God did not give you what you have so you could hoard it. He wants you to invest it in his kingdom, so you'll have wealth in this life and in the life to come.

Have you seen those exciting pro-life commercials with beautiful children playing? The television spots conclude with the statement, "Life — what a beautiful choice." If you'll notice the fine print, the commercial says it is sponsored by the Arthur DeMoss foundation. DeMoss was an insurance man God entrusted with a great fortune. His legacy is a foundation vested with 300 million dollars and one guiding principle: every dime of the interest on the foundation's investments is allocated to preaching the gospel of Jesus Christ. The resources God trusted to Arthur DeMoss are still blessing this nation, because God found an insurance man who said, "Lord, if you trust me with your resources, I'll bless this nation with the power of the gospel." And God said, "Open your hands, partner, here it comes."

How many of you feel like if you could get 300 million dollars together, you could trust God for the rest? Here's the point. If God gave you 300 million dollars it would probably destroy you, unless you were totally committed to investing it in the kingdom of God.

"Invest in yourselves." That's what this text says. "Lay up for yourselves treasures in heaven." God is not against treasure. He's just against investing in treasures that get away from you. He said, "Don't lay up treasures on earth where thieves carry it off and moths eat it and rust destroys it."

Jesus knew that you must learn to make your investments work for you. But many of you are so in debt that you have no savings and no investments. The Bible says to consider the example of the ant (Prov. 6:6-8). Every day the ant saves a portion of what it has for a future day. You should do the same thing.

Saving is a Bible principle. There will come a day

when you will need to draw from your resources, and if you have no investment, you have no future. That's what the Bible teaches.

Money never takes a day off

When you invest, your finances work for you 24 hours a day, 7 days a week, 365 days out of the year. Money never comes to you and says, "I'm emotionally drained. I need a four-week vacation in the Bahamas." Money never takes off sick and never comes to work late. Your finances will never join a union or need hospitalization. Money will only do what you tell it, when you tell it, like you tell it. The fact is, money will either enslave you or it will empower you.

Some young people are getting married and saying, "I want this, and I want this, and I want this, and I want this, because my mom and dad have all this." What you're forgetting is that it took them 30 years to put all that together. Don't get yourself so financially in hock over material possessions that you're screaming at each other in six months, "How are we going to pay for all this?"

Your investments reflect your interests. The Bible says that: "for where your treasure is, there will your heart be also." What are you interested in? Let's look at your checkbook and I can tell you exactly what you're interested in.

House payment $1,000
Tithe $10
Dog shampoo $50
TV ministry $5

Your checkbook shows you think 10 times as much of

your dog as you do preaching the gospel. That's a reflection of your heart.

If your investments are limited to this earth, you are the world's worst investor. The Bible says heaven and earth shall pass away. "The elements shall melt with fervent heat, the earth also and the works that are therein shall be burned up" (2 Peter 3:10). Some day this old world is going up in smoke, and all your earthly investments with it.

When you die, you're going to leave behind every penny you've ever made. How much money did Howard Hughes leave? All of it.

If I told you that your house would burn to the ground today by 12:00 noon, how many of you would go get everything you had and put it in the house? Would you leave your Mercedes in the garage? Would you go to the bank and get all of your stock certificates and put them in the house and say, "Wow! This will really make a great fire"? No, you'd do exactly the opposite. You would go get everything you had out of the house. You'd get all your friends to help you move your furniture and your clothes. You'd back your car out and remove all your valuable papers. You'd get it all out so it wouldn't burn up.

But some of you are investing everything you have right here on earth. The Bible says, "Don't invest it here, because it's going up in smoke." A man told me the other day, "Preacher, I'm not worried. I've moved my money from ABC Bank to XYZ Bank." Partner, moving your money from one bank to another in Texas is like shuffling deck chairs on the Titanic.

Eternal investments

So what do you do? You invest in the kingdom of God. That's the only eternal investment. God's not up for election every four years. He doesn't watch the Dow Jones ticker tape or read the Wall Street Journal. God says, "Give it to me. I'm your father. Let me invest it for you. I will give it back to you, good measure, pressed down, shaken together and running over. On top of that I'll throw in eternal life. I'll give you physical health. I'll give you love, joy and peace in the Holy Spirit. I'll even make your enemies to be at peace with you." Where can you match that?

There are two words that people confuse when they start talking about these things in the word of God. One is selfishness and the other is self-interest. Selfishness is cyanide. Selfishness will destroy you. It will bring destruction to your relationships and to the presence of God in your life. It is Satan's counterfeit for God's self-interest program.

Self-interest is not a sin. God is your Father and you're his child. He wants you to have the very best. "Beloved, I wish above all things that thou mayest prosper and be in health, even as thy soul prospereth" (3 John 2). When you become a child of God, God immediately wants you to do well. And the more you obey him, the better you do.

Salvation is in your self-interest. When you open this Book and read about hell, you'll not want to go there. I know some people tell you to go there all the time, because I've heard you talk. But hell is a real place; if you haven't received the Lord, that's where you're going. And contrary to popular rumor, it has not been air conditioned by the Southern Baptists or any other denomination.

Healing is in your self-interest. It's in your self-interest to have love, joy and peace in the Holy Spirit. These things are in your self-interest. But when you give yourself only to the things of the world, then that is selfishness and it will destroy you.

So Jesus' financial advice comes out this way: Invest in yourself, but invest wisely, because the final test of every investment is its permanence. Dewdrops are as pretty as diamonds — until the sun comes up. They're not permanent, they don't last. Jesus says not to invest on this earth because it's not permanent. Invest in his kingdom and he will give it back to you on both sides of the Jordan River.

"Lay up for yourselves treasures in heaven." Send it ahead of you, and it will be there when you get there. To the carnal mind that's insanity, because the carnal mind will only believe what it can see, touch and hold. But those who are persuaded that the word of God is true can firmly fix themselves upon the fact that the Lord is faithful, and he is a rewarder of those who diligently seek him.

The Bible says the final test of value is permanence. "He that doeth the will of God abideth for ever" (1 John 2:17). That's a powerful verse of scripture.

Somehow people get it in their minds that when they give money to the Lord, they'll never see it again. But that's the only money you're ever going to see again! There's a tombstone in England with this inscription:

What I spent, I lost.

What I kept, I lost.

What I gave, I now have.

Aren't we all going to have equal rewards in heaven? That's communism, not New Testament theology! The Bible says the first shall be last and the last shall be first. That's not equal. Rewards in heaven are directly proportionate to your service on earth. The Bible says our works will be tried by fire and some will "suffer loss" because their works will be burned up (1 Cor. 3:13-15). If you suffer loss, that's not an equal reward.

What you will have in heaven is directly proportionate to what you do on this earth. For some of you this is as close to heaven as you're going to get, because you have nothing over there to look forward to. Sacrifice in the Bible does not mean throwing something down the drain. That's a pagan mentality. Mothers in India may throw their children in the Ganges River and mothers in Africa may throw their babies to crocodiles in service to their gods. But Christians invest their lives in the kingdom of God, because it's the only kingdom that will endure.

What about the Lord's teachings on the deceitfulness of riches? Riches are deceitful. They appear to be what they are not. Riches appear to be security, but they are not. "For riches certainly make themselves wings; they fly away as an eagle toward heaven" (Prov. 23:5). Money talks all right: it says goodbye!

Riches appear to be a source of health and happiness, but they are not. Money can buy you a $50 steak, but only God can give you an appetite to enjoy it. Money buys associates, but it can't produce one true friend. Riches are deceitful. That's why you are not to lay up for yourselves treasures on earth, but in heaven.

Two kinds of investors

There are two kinds of investors here: reason investors and revelation investors. A reason investor is ruled by a carnal mind. He believes only what he can touch and taste and see. A revelation investor believes the word of God. He understands that the kingdom of God is like a treasure hidden in a field. He is willing to invest in what the carnal mind says is insanity, because he knows that in fact it is the only investment that will last.

The reason giver asks his accountant, "How much shall I give the Lord?" If the accountant gives too big a number, he gets fired. The revelation giver does not give based on what he has, he gives based on what God can supply — and there's no limit to it.

The widow who fed Elijah the last food she had in the house was a revelation giver. And while the king was walking the palace halls wondering where he was going to get his next meal, that widow had plenty because God replenished what she gave and added an abundant supply.

What is the return on your investment in the kingdom of God? Is it 10%, 20%, 50%? God gave a clear answer: "a hundredfold."

In Matthew 19, Jesus told his disciples that it is "easier for a camel to go through the eye of a needle, than for a rich man to enter into the kingdom of God" (verse 24). Simon Peter said, "Behold, we have forsaken all, and followed thee; what shall we have therefore?" (verse 27). Jesus did not say "Peter, shame on you for thinking you should get something back for following me. You should rejoice in your poverty." He didn't say that at all.

What he did say was this: "Verily I say unto you, that ye which have followed me, when the son of man shall sit in the throne of his glory, ye also shall sit upon twelve thrones, judging the twelve tribes of Israel" (verse 28). Think of that. He told the disciples they were going to leap from a dirty, smelly fishing boat with rotten nets to twelve thrones of glory. Do you see that as a promotion? That's really a nice leap forward.

And what's the return for the others who have followed Jesus? "And everyone that hath forsaken houses, or brethren, or sisters, or father, or mother, or wife, or children, or lands, for my name's sake, shall receive a hundredfold, and shall inherit everlasting life" (verse 29).

How much is a hundredfold? Is that 100%? No. One fold is 100%. A hundredfold is 10,000%. How would you like your investments to pay you 10,000%? That's what God says he will do for you.

How much shall I give the Lord? All that you want to get back. How much shall I keep? All that you want to lose. That's the bottom line.

The return is measured in more than dollars and cents. Listen to what I'm about to say here. All that God returns to you is not in money. That's a very shallow, ungodly, limited view. He brings it to you in health and in the power and purity of happy relationships.

When you invest for yourself with Jesus, he can make your enemies to be at peace with you. He can renew the relationships in your family that have been broken. He can give you peace that surpasses all understanding, and joy unspeakable and full of glory. He can take all that he has and give it to you, as long as he can trust you to invest in his kingdom.

Chapter 4
Success Without Stress

Our lives are dominated by clocks and calendars. We work in office buildings that are ulcer alleys. We drive in traffic jams that would make Job curse. Our cities have become asphalt jungles dominated by savages. Our homes are protected from those savages with burglar bars and alarms, dead bolts and dobermans. Many homeowners keep guns that are cocked and loaded.

This is a stressed-out society. We are filled with worry, anxiety and tension. It is the disease of the age.

Much of our stress we create ourselves. Mothers create stress when they worry about their children — what they're doing, what they're not doing, what they're learning, what they're not learning. There's not one marriage in this room that's not suffering from some degree of stress. There are businessmen in this room living on the naked edge, because stress has you by the throat. You've done everything you know to do in order to survive, yet your business is flitting through your hands like sand.

Jesus conducted a stress seminar in Matthew 6. Here's what he said:

> *Therefore I say unto you, Take no thought for your life, what ye shall eat, or what ye shall drink; nor yet for your body, what ye shall put on. Is not the life more than meat, and the body than raiment? Behold the fowls of the air: for they sow not, neither do they reap, nor gather into barns; yet your heavenly Father feedeth them. Are ye not much better than they? Which of you by taking thought can add one cubit unto his stature?*
>
> *And why take ye thought for raiment? Consider the lilies of the field, how they grow; they toil not, neither do they spin: And yet I say unto you, That even Solomon in all his glory was not arrayed like one of these. Wherefore, if God so clothe the grass of the field, which today is, and tomorrow is cast into the oven, shall he not much more clothe you, O ye of little faith? Therefore take no thought, saying, What shall we eat? or, What shall we drink? or, Wherewithal shall we be clothed? (For after all these things do the Gentiles seek:) for your heavenly Father knoweth that ye have need of all these things. But seek ye first the kingdom of God, and his righteousness; and all these things shall be added unto you. Take therefore no thought for the morrow: for the morrow shall take thought for the things of itself. Sufficient unto the day is the evil thereof.* (verses 25-34)

Jesus begins his seminar on stress by saying, "Take no thought for your life." We would say today, "Don't worry about life." Why should we not worry about life? Because God is our Father. He created us. He has given us everything we'll ever need. He takes care of the birds of the air and the flowers of the field, and He will take care of you.

The word of God is the manufacturer's manual for your heart, soul, mind and body. If you live according to its principles, there is never a reason for your life, your marriage, or your business to be dominated by stress. Today, tomorrow and forever He has the answer. Before you ever knew you had the need, God made the provision. He is the answer for your life, and He's the same yesterday, today and tomorrow.

Did you ever notice how worry always comes at a bad time? In every moment of crisis, just when you need a clear mind and steady nerves to make an important decision, here comes worry. Worry drains your creative energy and destroys your ability to come up with a better idea.

Worry will kill you

Worry and stress also happen to be killers. Stress makes cowards out of aggressive men. Worry fills the face with wrinkles and apprehension. Worry paralyzes the mind. Stress robs the body of rest at night, and it sends you to work shaking and shattered, incapable of solving the crises of the day.

Worry and stress are killing us. Worry is the mother of heart disease. Some doctors say that many forms of cancer are caused by the stressed-out society in which we live. Worry is the mother of high blood pressure and ulcers. It's not what you're eating, it's what's eating you that's the problem.

Jesus said, "Don't worry." Worry has sent millions

of people to their graves years before they were supposed to die. People who were supposed to have known the Prince of Peace. Jesus said not to worry. "Take no thought for tomorrow. I have taken care of it. I will never leave you. I will never forsake you. Don't worry."

Worry is sin. Worry is faith in fear. God has not given us a spirit of fear (2 Tim. 1:7). Fear is Satan's trademark — and if you're living in fear, you're not dominated by the Prince of Peace.

Worry is trust in the unpleasant. Worry is assurance that disaster is going to overtake you. Worry is belief in defeat and despair. The apostle of worry says, "Because of the bomb ... because of Saddam Hussein ... because of pollution ... because of the IRS ... because of PMS, I have no future." Do you think like that? Do you talk like that? Then you are the apostle of worry.

Worry is a stream that surges through your mind, drowning hope, drowning faith, drowning optimism. Worry is interest paid on trouble before you it happens. One old man said, "Most of the trouble I've had in life never happened." But how many of you are worried about something that's going to happen in your life in the next few days? You're just sure it's going to happen, although it hasn't happened yet, and you're sure it's not going to be pleasant. Jesus said, "Don't worry about life."

What do we worry about? We worry about things we can't change. Husbands worry about what their wives spend. They worry about what the government spends. (The difference is they're not afraid to criticize the government.) We worry about being unfavorably compared with somebody else. The Bible says not to compare yourselves among yourselves. Wife, there will always be somebody prettier than you. Husband, there will always be somebody more handsome than you. There will always be a better salesman, a better lawyer, a better doctor, a better preacher. Be happy with where you are and who you are. God made you what you are — be glad with that.

I think all class reunions, whether high school or college, are nothing but comparison carnivals. You left 30 years ago young, healthy, happy and beautiful, and you come back bald as a billiard table, with bulges and bifocals and bunions all over your body. What's fun about that? The absolute joy is finding that the man who was voted most likely to succeed, didn't ... and the girl who was voted Most Beautiful now looks like a mobile home in a skirt. Stop comparing yourselves among yourselves. When you were conceived in your mother's body, something called a genetic code took over, and there's nothing you can ever do to change that. Nothing. So quit worrying about it. Don't worry about what you can't change. Don't worry about what you can change — just change it. If it's bothering you, change it. But don't worry, because it's an absolute waste of time.

Don't worry about what to eat and drink

God's word says, "Don't worry about food, don't worry about fashions, and don't worry about the future." Some of the wealthiest people I know are afraid they are going to run out of something to eat, something to drink, or something to wear. Have you ever asked a fat man for directions? He'll say, "Go past McDonald's and turn left, go two blocks, turn right at Little Caesar's, and you'll find what you're looking for next door to Luby's." He's obsessed with what he's going to eat. There are people all over the world who are worried about food. God is saying, "I'm in the food business. For 40 years I catered meals to the children of Israel in the wilderness. I rained manna in the morning, and gave them water out of the rock. I fed Elijah angel food cake. I fed 5,000 out of one boy's sack lunch."

The Lord's prayer says, "Give us this day our daily bread." I want you to hear this. America could have a food crisis. In the 1980s foreign countries bought up much of our agricultural land. The family farm is dead in America, and the corporate farms are now in charge of food production. If you know anything about European history, you know that what brought about the great starvation of the 1920s was the collapse of the family farm. We could easily have a food crisis here in America, where every person in this country gets down on his knees and literally prays, "Give us this day our daily bread." Am I worried? No way. Donald Trump may starve to death on the doorstep of the Rockefellers, but I will not go hungry. God Almighty is my provider, and he told me not to worry about having something to eat.

Jesus also told us not to worry about having something to drink. Why did Jesus teach us not to worry about water? In every American home there are 15 faucets, sprinklers in the yard to water the grass, and shower stalls that would make Pharoah jealous. My wife doesn't take a shower, she takes a vertical swim.

Jesus' instruction not to worry about water is even more compelling when you consider that in Israel, then and now, water is very scarce. There is only one water supply, the Sea of Galilee. Why did Jesus spend two-thirds of his ministry around the Sea of Galilee? Because that's where the water was, and water kept the people alive. When you walk through the streets of Jerusalem you see huge water cisterns that have been chiseled in the rock beneath the street. Those cisterns hold millions of gallons of water. When the Romans attacked Jerusalem, when the Crusaders attacked Jerusalem, and in the war of independence in 1948 when the Arabs attacked Jerusalem, those water cisterns gave the city the life and the vitality to keep from being conquered by their enemies. General Ariel Sharon once told me that the six-day war in 1967 was started over water. You certainly didn't read that in the newspaper here. The Syrians used bulldozers to re-route the three rivers that supply the Sea of Galilee. The result was instant war.

Without water, there are no crops. Without crops, there is no money and no food, and ultimately, there is famine and death. So when Jesus said, "I have the ability to supply water," he hit their hot button. The message here is that God can supply what you need, when you need it. And he can supply all that you need.

Are you worried about your finances? Do not, for "my God shall supply all your need according to his riches in glory by Christ Jesus" (Phil. 4:19). I assure you, the gates of heaven have not been hocked by Wall Street. Are you worried about your enemies? Do not, for "greater is he that is in you, than he that is in the world" (1 John 4:4). The Bible says that God will make my enemies to be at peace with me (Prov. 16:7). Nobody has a public relations firm that can do that. But the Lord can.

Are you living your life shackled by fear? Do not be mastered by fear. Do not be mastered by stress, for the Lord is the strength of your life. Don't worry about your health. He is the Great Physician, and he still makes house calls. Don't worry about life. "I am come that they might have life, and that they might have it more abundantly" (John 10:10). Don' worry about death. "I am he that liveth, and was dead; and, behold, I am alive for evermore, Amen" (Rev. 1:18). Don't worry about life, don't worry about death. Don't worry about the past, don't worry about the future. Don't worry about anything, period, because the Lord your God will meet every need, when you need it, like you need it, to the fullest extent you will ever need it.

The agnostic says, "Well, we really don't need to depend on anything as emotional as God to supply our needs." Scientists claim we now have the ability through technology to seed the clouds and it will rain whenever we want it to. But when there was a drought in Georgia, the farmers didn't go to Harvard to get rain. They went to the house of God and knelt down and asked him to send rain. When the lights in New York City failed because of a computer glitch, the brightest minds in the industry sat there and waited until God's power and light company — which is called the sun — came back on line. Without the help of our technology, the sun still rises every morning. People in California have to wait until the breeze from the ocean blows the smog away. For all of our brilliance, we have not replaced our need of the Living God. He is the one who gives the rain. He's the one who gives the air. He is the one who gives the plants we eat, and without him we can't take our next breath.

Don't worry about what to wear

Jesus said not to worry about food, and he said not to worry about fashion. "Why take ye thought for raiment (clothing)?" (Matt. 6:28). When Jesus sent his disciples out, he told them to take only one change of clothes

(Luke 9:3). On top of that, he said that if they met someone on the way that had no coat, to give him theirs (Luke 6:29). Jesus was not concerned about having a big wardrobe. Mother Teresa says all she needs is a dress to wear, a dress to wash, and a dress to mend. Yet American Christians are obsessed with appearance. We are into "body ministry." We feed the body, we rest the body, we put the body in a nice car, we take the body on a nice cruise to the Bahamas, we decorate the body with various colors of paint, we pamper the body, we massage the body with grease at night. You squeeze your wife, she squirts into the next room like a seed out of a lemon. But no matter how much you try to improve on Mother Nature, you cannot fool Father Time.

Americans think we just have to be in style. We cannot simply have something that adorns us properly, it must be what Madison Avenue says is correct. This may be my German nature, but I'm sick and tired of Madison Avenue jerking us around. Just about the time you get your closet filled with what you're supposed to look like, then they shorten the length of the skirt, or they drop it to the floor, or the tie goes from something that looks like a shoestring to something that looks like a tablecloth. I've had some ties for so long that they've been in style five times. 1 Peter 3 says don't be adorned with fancy garments, but be adorned in your heart with the "ornament of a meek and quiet spirit, which is in the sight of God of great price" (3:3-4).

There is something more important in the mission of the church than how we appear. Looking good is wonderful — do the best with what you have, and God bless you for the effort. But what we're about here is not fashion and food. What we're about here is the winning of the lost. What we're about here is world evangelism.

What we're about here is healing the sick ... breaking the chains of addiction ... conquering demon powers ... preaching the gospel of Jesus Christ. Gucci can't bring this nation back again, but God can. And that's what the church is all about.

It is a brutal fact that your body is a lump of dirt. When you stop breathing, you're going to fall in a hole and become a banquet for worms. That's realism. Get it in your mind that there's something more important than how you look. Whenever Jesus preached, he didn't jump out of a boat wearing a sequin suit with a pinky ring and patent leather shoes and Bible to match. Peter didn't grab the microphone and say, "Heeeeere's Jesus." The church in America needs to get its priorities right. Don't worry about the future. And don't worry about what you're going to eat or what you're going to wear.

You're not an orphan

Here are the reasons why you should not worry. Number one: do not worry, because God is your father.

Do you really believe that? When I was a youngster, I worked in an orphanage in Houston, Texas. Orphans have an insecurity that I don't think they ever really shake. They're constantly looking for a father figure to fill that vacancy in their hearts. During the second world war there was an orphanage in Europe where the children were happy and well-adjusted, while the children in other orphanages were tormented. The U. S. government sent an inspection team to find out what made this orphanage different. They found a grandmother and grandfather who had taken in all these children. At night they would roll up one slice of bread and put it in the hand of each child. They put them to bed with a good night kiss and told them that everything would be all right tomorrow. Clutching that piece of bread, reassured that they were loved and cared for, those children could sleep through the bombs falling, while children in the other orphanages cried and screamed day and night.

That is a metaphor for our lives. God the Father has taken this loaf of bread and placed it in your hand, and He said, "I will be your burden bearer. I will provide every crumb of bread you need to eat. Everything you ever thought you would have need of, I will give it to you. I am the God of all hope. I want you to look at tomorrow with optimism. If people are running you out of town, get in front of the group and make it look like a parade, because you're my child. Rejoice and be exceedingly glad, because I'm your father. You're not a spiritual orphan."

Another reason not to worry is that worry absolutely produces nothing.

Jesus said worrying cannot add one cubit to your stature (Matt. 6:27). A cubit is about 18 inches, roughly the distance from the tip of your finger to your elbow. Now if I could add 18 inches to my height by worrying, I'd start worrying right now. That would make me 7' 2". I'd sign up with the Spurs and be part of the "dream team." But that's not going to happen. The Greek word translated stature is *helikia*, which can also mean "length of life." So Jesus asked, "Which of you by worrying can lengthen your life?" You cannot.

Americans are doing everything possible to lengthen their lives. They're taking all sorts of vitamins that you can get from natural foods, but that's not good enough. So they're taking megadoses of vitamin pills. They jog.

They jog in the rain, they jog in the sleet, they jog in the snow; they won't go to church if it's overcast, but they'll jog into a hurricane. Exercise is great, but it won't necessarily lengthen your life.

The Great Physician, the master architect of the body, said this machine is not designed to worry because the manufacturer has taken care of every need that it will ever have. Jesus then gave two illustrations: sparrows and grass.

Learn from the birds

He said, "Consider the sparrows. The sparrows do not drink Maalox. They do not read the *Wall Street Journal* or *Better Homes and Gardens*. Yet I attend the funeral of every sparrow that falls. Are you not much more valuable than they? If I take care of the sparrows, won't I take care of you?" Sparrows do not sow, they do not reap, they do not gather into barns. Sparrows do not have conferences and say, "This is how we're going to increase production next year." But God feeds them.

If God takes care of the birds, he'll take care of you. Some people hear what Jesus said and they say, "That's for me. I'm not going to work. I'm going to climb a tree and open my mouth." The fact is, God provides worms for birds, but he does not throw them down their throats. Worry kills more people than work. Some of you are playing it safe and doing neither. Birds don't read books about how to relax. They don't say, "Next year, bird, we're going to eat, drink and be merry." Birds do not overindulge. They only get fat when someone — man — puts them in cages.

Men, on the other hand, get greedy. They ignore

God's provision while they stockpile and hoard and accumulate wealth. Then they start depending on Maalox to get them through the day and Valium to get them through the night. They live on the naked edge and their homes are living war zones, all because they're afraid somebody's going to get all they have. Finally, when men get their bodies and minds so wired that they can't lie down at night, then they go to the sporting goods store, buy an expensive set of binoculars, and go out in the country and watch the birds — the birds who know that God will take care of them, that God will protect them, and God will provide for them.

Are you as smart as a bird? Then why are you dominated by stress? Stop worrying. In Jesus' name, take every care you have and give it to the Lord.

Chapter 5
Success Through Excellence

There is a story about an American Indian who found an eagle's egg and placed it in the nest of a prairie chicken. The eaglet hatched with a brood of prairie chickens and grew up with them. Thinking he was a prairie chicken, the eagle did what the other prairie chickens did. He scratched in the dirt for seeds and worms. He clucked and he cackled. He never flew more than a few feet, because that's what the prairie chickens did. One day he saw a magnificent bird, flying gracefully and effortlessly far above him in the cloudless sky. On the powerful wind currents it soared majestically with scarcely a beat of its mighty wings. The earth-bound eagle asked the prairie chickens, "What is that beautiful bird?" The prairie chickens said, "That's the eagle. He is the chief of birds. But you could never fly like him, because you're just a prairie chicken." So the eagle never gave it another thought and eventually he died, deceived and deprived of his heritage because he was persuaded by the limited vision of others. God had designed him to soar into the heavens. He was destined for high adventure. Yet he pecked at seeds and scratched the dirt, cackling and clucking, convinced he was only a prairie chicken. What a waste.

The greater waste is that millions of Christians — designed by the Creator to fly to the highest heights of heaven and to sit in the heavenlies with him — are scratching in the dirt for seeds and worms, cackling and clucking, convinced that they're just prairie chickens. What about you? Do you see yourself as God sees you, as a divine creation, designed to soar with excellence into the highest realms of accomplishment? Are you an earth-bound prairie chicken, scratching for seeds and worms, or a spiritual eagle who knows the joy of reaching for heaven's best and living in the dimension of excellence?

"They that wait upon the Lord shall renew their strength; they shall mount on wings of eagles," Isaiah 40:31 says. But if you've adopted the prairie chicken mentality, if you have given up on your dreams and hopes, you'll never know what could have been possible if you had only dared to try. Don't be persuaded by the opinions of the prairie chickens around you, when God has designed you to be an eagle.

God's will for you is excellence

It is God's will for you to achieve excellence. St. Paul prayed for the Philippian believers that they would learn to "approve things that are excellent" (Phil. 1:10). David wrote of "the saints that are in the earth ... the excellent" (Psalm 16:3). God considers you, his saints, the excellent ones. Peter instructed the early church to "add to your faith virtue" (2 Peter 1:5). Virtue is excellence. The point Peter is making here is that we should add excellence to our faith. God is saying to the saints, "I want you to grow ... stretch ... reach for new horizons." There's more to being a Christian than going to church on Sunday. There's more to being a Christian than just going to heaven. There is the dimension of adding to your faith excellence and being all you can be by the grace of God.

There's an appalling lack of excellence in America. Our industrial leadership has been lost because we have abandoned our commitment to excellence. Our schools are producing graduates who can't read, can't write and can't spell, because excellence is no longer our goal. If a foreign government had done to our educational system what America's educators have done, we would consider it an act of war.

There's an appalling lack of excellence in moral standards. We have gone from Ozzie and Harriett to Woody Allen and Mia Farrow. We have gone from love to lust. We have gone from covenant to convenience. We have gone from fidelity to fornication. It's time for America to return to the excellence of the word of God in preserving and protecting family values.

There's an appalling lack of excellence in the body of Christ. Sloppy agape is a fact, not fiction. Church leaders have stopped using words like duty and discipline and discipleship. But excellence in your life remains a basic form of Christian witnessing. Every job is the portrait of the man or the woman who does it. Whether you paint houses or preach sermons, whether you sell steamships or shoelaces, your job performance is a reflection of your Christian belief. If you try to witness to your neighbor across the fence while your unmowed yard is filled with junk and trash, do God a favor and tell your neighbor you're an atheist. Tell them you're with Madelyn O'Hair or Shirley MacLaine. Don't tell them you're with God, because junk and trash are not what God is all about. Paul said in Colossians 3, "Whatsoever ye do in word or deed, do all in the name of the of the Lord Jesus" (v. 17) and "Whatsoever ye do, do it heartily, as to the Lord, and not unto men" (v. 23). "Whatsoever ye do, do all to the glory of God" (1 Cor. 10:31). The message is this: either do it with excellence or don't do it at all.

What is it that God has given you to do? To be a home minister? Then do it with excellence, or don't do it at all. To sing in the choir? Then do it with excellence Sunday after Sunday. To be a Sunday School teacher, an usher, a greeter, a telephone counselor, an attorney, a doctor, a salesman, a housewife, an educator? Whatever you do, do it with excellence. Don't wish for your job to be easier. If it was, everybody would be doing it and you would be unemployed. Ask God to kill that prairie chicken attitude you've got, that sloppy, slovenly attitude that allows you to accept mediocrity instead of the best. If you're going fishing for Moby Dick, take the tartar sauce with you!

Reasons we fail to achieve excellence

Why don't we achieve excellence? One reason is that we waste time. The Bible very plainly says in Ephesians 5:15, "Redeem the time." We don't achieve excellence because we waste our lives one minute at a time. Time cannot be stored ... it cannot be stopped ... and it cannot be borrowed. We all wake up every morning with the same amount of time allotted to us. If you do not control your time, you're out of control of your life. David said in Psalm 37:23, "The steps of a good man are ordered by the Lord." Every day should have a plan. Quit living your life willy nilly and start living by divine appointment. When you get up in the morning have something that's on God's agenda, and do that.

Here's a tip from the President of U. S. Steel, who paid $25,000 for advice on how to be more productive. This is the plan the experts devised for him. Every night, before you go to bed, list the ten most important things you have to do the next day, in order of their importance. Then when you get up the next morning, start doing them systematically. Plan your work and work your plan. Killing time is suicide to success. When you kill time, it's gone forever. My father used to say this to his four sons quite often: "I only want you boys to work a half day, and I don't care which 12 hours you choose." He was very serious about that.

Psalm 90:12 says, "Teach us to number our days, that we may apply our hearts unto wisdom." On judgment day, you and I are going to stand before God and answer for the gap that exists between where we are and where we could have been had we lived by God's plan, had we been willing to crucify that prairie chicken mentality and be all that God wanted us to be. Why don't we achieve excellence? Because we have a limited vision of what God can do through us. If God could use a crooked stick in the hand of Moses to lead Israel out of Egypt's bondage, if he could use a rooster to preach a message of conviction to Peter, if he could use a donkey to preach to Balaam, then he can use me and he can use you. Quit going around whining with that brood of prairie chickens you hang out with and start recognizing that you can fly and do impossible things, because "greater is he that is in you than he that is in the world" (1 John 4:4). Dream a new dream. Catch a new vision of who you are. Fly on the wings of faith. Dare to go further than your natural eyes can see. Nothing is impossible to those who believe.

Remember, good is the enemy of better, and better is the enemy of best. You can't have something better until you let go of what you consider good. Don't let some old prairie chicken talk you out of God's best. That's what prairie chickens do. "Oh praise God, aren't these bugs delicious? Aren't we humble, digging for worms in the dirt?" Don't listen to the stupid drivel of prairie chickens. Take yourself out behind the barn and give yourself a swift kick. Get angry with your half-baked, mediocre approach to life and get out of the rut. Do something different, even if you do it wrong. Decide to live with enthusiasm, vigor, accomplishment, direction and excellence.

What is your dream? Whatever it is, however impossible it seems, if it is noble, if it is consistent with the word of God, if it fits the purposes of God for your life, then lock your jaws onto it like a bulldog and go for it. Do not stop. Do not quit. Do not compromise. Make it happen. Live in the dimension of excellence, because that's the mark of a child of God.

Fear of success and fear of failure

We fail to reach greatness because we fear success. People are afraid that if they do well, if they buy a better house or a better car, then their friends will talk bad about them or won't like them any more. Wrong. Your friends will be glad. Those prairie chickens you're running around with, they're the ones who will be upset. They're the ones who will talk about you. Quit worrying about the vision and the opinion of the prairie chickens around you. If they can only fly ten feet and you can go further, then fly as far as you can. God has engineered you to fly. If others are willing to live in the prison of fear and doubt, don't let them dominate your life.

Another reason we do not reach excellence is because of our fear of failure. Failure is a better teacher than success. Every great success story has its element of failure. You have not failed until you quit; only then have you failed. After Thomas Edison finished his 700th experiment trying to develop the electric light his assistant said, "We have failed." Edison replied, "No. We have found 700 ways that will not work. Do not call these 700 experiments mistakes; call them our education. Now let's keep going until we find the answer." Are you afraid of failure? Then you'll never succeed. You'll never stub your toe standing still. Remember the turtle: He never gets anywhere until he sticks his neck out. You can't succeed if you're not willing to risk failure.

Ted Williams, one of the greatest baseball players of all time, had a batting average of .400. For those of you who don't stay up with baseball, that means that four out of ten times when he came up to bat, he got on base. And that figure made him the all-time batting champion in baseball. But it also means that he failed to get on base six out of ten times. Even if you fail six out of ten times, in professional baseball you can renegotiate your contract — that's what that says.

Have you failed? Get up. Wipe the dust and the dirt off of your face. Get back in the race. Don't give an alibi, give it another try. Failure is not the worst thing in the world that could happen to you. The very worst thing in the word is your refusal to try again. One of my favorite quotes is from Theodore Roosevelt, who said, "Far better it is to dare mighty things, to win glorious triumphs, even though checkered by failure, than to take rank with those poor spirts who neither enjoy much nor suffer much, because they live in the gray twilight that knows not victory nor defeat."

Excellence overcomes handicaps

Excellence is not determined by sex, age, race, or occupation. Don't make excuses or plead your limitations. Everybody is handicapped in some ways. You can use your handicap as an excuse to scratch in the dirt with prairie chickens, or you can use it as a motivation to fly into the heavens and be all you can be.

Moses was handicapped. He said to God, "I can't lead these people, I'm slow of speech." Joseph was handicapped. He was a foreigner, an ex-con fresh out of jail, yet God made him one of the most powerful men in Egypt, second only to Pharaoh. Paul was handicapped. He spoke of a thorn in his side. Paul wrote most of the New Testament — and most of it was written while he was in jail.

A 12-year old boy was so badly burned in a school fire that the doctor said he would never walk again. That boy not only wanted to walk, he wanted to be a track star. He pushed himself to excellence by learning to walk again, stretching the scar tissue that hurt his legs. And in 1934 the world watched Glenn Cunningham as he broke the world's record by running a mile in 4 minutes and 6 seconds. How was he able to go from not being able to walk to being the world's fastest runner? He wouldn't listen to the prairie chickens who told him he couldn't do it.

Another reason we fail to achieve excellence is lack of discipline. Discipline yourself so other people won't have to, and that's good whether you're 15 or 45. There is no discipleship without discipline. Church, it's time to leave sloppy agape and come to discipline and discipleship. The Bible says, "Be thou faithful unto death" (Rev. 2:10). Paul said to endure hardship as a good soldier (2 Tim. 2:3). Quit living by your emotions. You will only reach for excellence living by duty and discipline and discipleship.

We also fail to achieve excellence because we've become so sensitive. We're environmentally sensitive. There are people in this country more sensitive about spotted owls than they are about unborn human beings. They'll climb a tree to keep you from taking the life of an owl while demanding that every woman be allowed to abort the baby in her womb. We're economically sensitive. We try to keep up with the Joneses, and when we can't, we put on airs. We become pretentious; the Bible calls it hypocrisy.

We've become racially sensitive. We've come up with a new name for everybody because we don't want to offend anybody. I have taken to calling my dog a Canine American. Indians are no longer Indians, they're Native Americans. Mexicans are no longer Mexicans, they're Hispanics. Black people are now African Americans or "people of color." White people, according to Hollywood, are the people who can't jump. My daughter and I were watching the Olympics and she looked at me in absolute innocence and said, "Dad, why can't white people run faster?" I said, "Sandy, I don't know. But they can't jump either, so just watch your step."

The Bible says it is God's desire for you to live in excellence. He wants you to mount on the wings of eagles and reach for greatness. Some of you will never enjoy success through excellence because you have been satisfied with something far less than what God has designed for you. You do not see yourself as God sees you. You see yourself in the reflection of the prairie chickens around you. You're satisfied to scratch for bugs and worms in bitter frustration. I'd rather try something big and fail than to plan to do nothing and to succeed. Reach for the excellence that's in God's will for you.

Chapter 6

Success Through Perseverance

There comes a time in every life when quitting looks good, when the problems seem insurmountable, when the giants seem unbeatable, and when defeat seems inescapable. There comes a time in every job when quitting looks good. Every job has its drudgery, its sweat and toil; not every day is a holiday. There comes a time in every marriage when quitting looks good, when "for better or for worse" just seems to be more than you bargained for.

But God is able to make us always triumph through Jesus Christ (2 Cor. 2:14). The Bible says that nothing is impossible to those who believe (Mark 9:23), and that all things will work out for our good when we are called according to the purposes of God (Romans 8:28).

The point is, if you're going to succeed in life, you must learn the power of persistence. Life does not consist of doing what you want to do. Life consists of doing what you ought to do. Duty requires discipline, and success comes to those with the daring to pursue the purposes of God, to those who endure to the end in those causes to which God has called them.

Jesus is our example of endurance and perseverance. "Looking unto Jesus the author and finisher of our faith; who for the joy that was set before him endured the cross, despising the shame, and is set down at the right hand of the throne of God" (Hebrews 12:2).

There is power in persistence. Nothing great in your life is ever going to happen without persistence. There is nothing half-hearted or lukewarm about persistence. Persistence is bold. Persistence is fearless. Persistence does not look over its shoulder at yesterday's mistakes. Persistence is not manipulated by the lie that I must have everyone's approval to succeed.

There are two kinds of people the world will never tolerate: those who succeed and those who fail. If you succeed, people will say, "He was a cheater and a thief." If you fail, they'll say, "If the lazy deadbeat would have gotten up and gone to work, better things would have happened for him." If you think you're going to be unusual and the world will applaud you, you are living in an illusion. Persistence does not play the blame game, blaming unhappiness or failure on others.

Persistence is the divine fire that burns in your bones with a white hot intensity that hell and high water can't put out. Jesus told us to endure, to persist, to persevere. He said that a man who puts his hand to the plow and then looks back is not worthy of the kingdom (Luke 9:62). He says to press on. Learn to endure. Learn to persevere until you accomplish the purposes of God.

We are more than conquerors

St. Paul, who said we are more than conquerors through Christ (Romans 8:37), was the apostle of persistence. Did he say this when everything was going smoothly and he had no reason for discouragement? No, he said "we are more than conquerors" after being beaten three times with a Roman cat-of-nine tails ... after being stoned and left for dead in the dirt ... after being betrayed by his dearest friends ... after living in the hell of constant accusation year in and year out ... after he was marched from one penitentiary to another in handcuffs ... after being shipwrecked ... after writing to the New Testament church, "Don't be ashamed of the Lord, or me his prisoner" (2 Tim. 1:8). That's when he wrote that we are more than conquerors through Christ.

He had walked through the fire, but the fire didn't burn him. He had walked through the water, but the water didn't drown him. He was bitten by a deadly viper but he shook that snake off and kept on pursuing the purposes of God. He didn't whine and he didn't resign. He pressed "toward the mark for the prize of the high calling of God in Christ Jesus" (Phil. 3:14).

I dare say that none of you here this week have been beaten with a Roman cat-of-nine tails, nor stoned and left for dead. But Paul, when these things happened to him, said, "These light afflictions, which last only a moment, will achieve eternal glory for us" (2 Cor. 4:17). In America these days, if you speak to someone about their Christian faith and it's just not glowing and oozing with complimentary overtones, they're highly offended. Christians in the early church were thrown to the lions in the Roman coliseum and they rejoiced that they were counted worthy to know Jesus Christ as Lord and

Savior. Listen to the words of Paul: "We are hard pressed on every side, but not crushed; perplexed, but not in despair; persecuted, but not abandoned; struck down, but not destroyed" (2 Cor. 4:8). The Hagee translation reads like this: "Hell has thrown the kitchen sink at us but we're still on our feet, fighting the good fight of faith. We will endure and we will be triumphant through Christ the Lord." And shortly before his head was chopped off, this prophet of persistence put his pen to parchment and wrote, "I have fought a good fight, I have finished my course, I have kept the faith: Henceforth there is laid up for me a crown of righteousness ... and not to me only, but unto all them also that love his appearing" (2 Tim. 4:7-8).

Have you been knocked down? Has a bitter divorce left you flat of your back and absolutely devoid of self-significance? Have you lost a dear loved one in death? Have you been knocked down by a financial reversal? Are you suffering through a bankruptcy? Has your dearest friend knocked you down with accusations? Have those who have loved you in times past now started to attack you? I have a message from St. Paul: Get up! In Jesus' name, dust yourself off and get back in the race.

Falling down does not make you a failure. Staying down makes you a failure. If you get up one more time than you're knocked down, you're the winner. I like the word triumph: "try-umph"! Get up again and give it another shot. Don't give me an alibi, give it another try, in Jesus' name. Winston Churchill said that the nose of a bulldog is sloped back so he can bite and breathe without turning loose. God give us bulldog believers so anointed with the Holy Spirit that hell's legions tremble whenever we turn over in bed — not some whiny group of Bible-thumping wimps who are so sensitive they can't endure a little bit of the pressure of life.

Persistence produces success. President Calvin Coolidge said, "Nothing in the world can take the place of persistence. Talent will not; nothing is more common than unsuccessful men with talent. Education will not; the world is full of educated derelicts. Persistence and determination alone are omnipotent. The slogan 'press on' has solved and always will solve the problems of the human race."

Do you have persistence? Without it your dreams are an illusion. Without it your plans are a hoax and your hopes are an absolute pipe dream. The story of Jacob wrestling with the angel all night is a story of persistence. Jacob said, "I will not let you go except you bless me." Because of that encounter, he walked with a limp for the rest of his life. But he got his blessing, and was renamed "prince of God" to boot. The difference in being a prince with God and a common drifter is simply persistence.

God wants persistent plodders

In the book of Ezekiel, God presents the four faces of the man of God. These are the four characteristics of those who serve the Lord. The first is the face of the lion. The righteous are as bold as a lion, the Bible says (Prov. 28:1). If you're not bold, then you're not righteous. The second face is that of an eagle. Those who wait upon the Lord "shall renew their strength; they shall mount up with wings as eagles" (Isa. 40:31) and sail into the very presence of the living God. The third face is the face of a man, because you will always be a human being, no matter how spiritual you think you are.

The fourth face is that of an ox, which brings me to the point of the sermon: An ox is a persistent plodder. When you feed an ox, it does not bray like a donkey. It just gets out and plows. Give it some oats and it will plow, plow, plow. More oats, plow, plow. No bellyaching, it just plods and plows ... and plods and plows ... and plods and plows. Let me tell you something, friend. God is not looking for flash and dash. He's looking for persistent plodders. Those with flash and dash will fall in the ditch. God is looking for the oxen who will put their shoulders to the wheel and pull, who are committed to duty, committed to discipline, determined to finish the race. God is looking for men and women who will be divine, persistent plodders to pursue the purposes of God.

Perseverance is the portrait of the saints. How can you tell who's a Christian? Certainly not by what they say. You can talk the talk and not walk the walk. Certainly not by what they write. If the glowing reports on the fly pages of every religious book were true, the devil would be in the back end of hell drinking Maalox and waving a white flag, screaming, "No more!" So how can you tell who's a Christian? The Bible gives the answer: *by their fruit.* Fruit cannot be produced in a day. Fruit cannot be produced in a week. Fruit takes months and years to come to maturity. The point is, you can't tell who is a persistent Christian until you have seen their fruit, and that takes time. Only the persistent will produce fruit.

Cornerstone Church is an orchard bearing much fruit. It did not begin late last night. It began on Mother's Day 1975. It has been built through the blood, sweat, tears and perseverance of godly men and women who refused to compromise with the world, the flesh and the devil. A pastor who was visiting this church from out of state said to me, "You really have it nice here. How'd you get started?" His implication was that a major denomination funded me and our church just exploded. Well, that's not how we got started. It started with me living in the garage of a church member for one year. Not garage apartment, just the garage; they moved the car out and I moved in. I shared that garage with a companion, a 125-pound great dane. Never have liked dogs since then. My vast wardrobe was hanging on a 1" piece of pipe in the back corner of the garage.

But things got better. We got the church going and I moved into the missionary quarters: a 10x12 room with its own electric heater. Big time. Big bucks, too. I made $7,000 every year for three years in a row, and knew I was lucky to get it. Then I got married. My wife was Hispanic (for you Bubbas out there, that's Mexican), and we found out that racism is alive and well in the church. We had a new minister of education named Rick Randall who kept a chart of our church growth, and the line just went straight down. He said, "What can I do to explain this line?" I said, "Write on that line FLEW EPIDEMIC." Many members flew the coop, but we're still here, praise God.

I've been shot at point blank — in church, in front of the congregation — by a demonized lunatic under the control of witchcraft. I've had investigative reporters dig through my past like maggots on a corpse. I've been cussed and discussed, analyzed and scandalized. The devil's mad and I'm glad. The battle rages, and that's just how I like it. Our church has put hell on notice. We're not here to get along to go along. We're here to fight the good fight of faith. We're here to lift the bloodstained banner of Jesus Christ up until the nations of the world confess that Jesus is Lord to the glory of God the Father. We're on the attack. We have put on the whole armor of God, and in the power of Jesus' name we are attacking the gates of hell. We've served notice on the devil, "Come out wherever you are, because we're going to run the sword of righteousness through your hide until you look like Swiss cheese on the hoof — the victory is ours through Jesus Christ the Lord."

Perhaps you have been struggling to make your dreams come true. You're tired, exhausted, on the very brink of depression. Quitting looks good right now. I'm saying to you in Jesus' name, don't do it. Press on. Endure. Try again. Fight back. Christ is our example. Jesus, the author and finisher of our faith, endured the cross. Calvary is not the name of a picnic ground outside the eastern wall of Jerusalem. It's where the son of God fought the most vicious battle in the history of the world. He did not quit. He did not surrender. He endured the cross and gave me the victory over death, hell and the grave. And because he endured, you can endure. Nothing is impossible to those who know the Lord Jesus and are called according to the purposes of God.

Be faithful unto death

There's joy in enduring. There's joy in beating the problem to a pulp. There's joy in putting your foot on the neck of your enemy. There's joy in standing in the winner's circle with the gold around your neck. You may be there with blood and dirt on your face, but you are a child of God and persistence is in your bloodline. The word of God says, "Be thou faithful unto death" (Rev.

2:10). Unto death — not until someone insults you, not until you get your feelings hurt, but when you die — then you can stop being faithful.

Persistence is Abraham looking for a city whose builder and maker was God, and not finding it until he died and saw the Lord. Persistence is Noah building an ark for 120 years without a Black &Decker saw, without approval from OSHA, without a government grant — and the thing floated. Persistence is Job attending the funeral of his children, watching his wealth vanish, his health failing, and listening to his sharp-tongued wife who told him to curse God and die. But Job said, "Though he slay me, yet will I trust in him" (Job 13:15). Job was determined to endure.

Persistence is a decision. You're not born with persistence, you decide to be persistent. Show me somebody who loses gracefully, and I'll show you a loser. You lose by being willing to lose. Matthew 24;13 says, "But he that shall endure unto the end, the same shall be saved." Who is the winner in the Olympics? Not the one who starts, the one who finishes. The starting gun is fired and they all begin to run. Sweat pours down their faces. Tiredness sets in as they strain toward the finish line. Exhaustion overtakes one and he drops out. Another trips and falls. Each runner feels the lungs burning, trying to get more air. Finally, one crosses the finish line. Who is it that wins? He that endures to the end.

Finish what you start. Don't let your life be just beginnings and there's never a conclusion to anything. Finish! A child of God endures and finishes his assignment. The worst failures in history are those who began well but could not finish what God gave them to do.

Judas Iscariot began as a disciple of Jesus Christ. He heard the teaching. He saw the miracles. But in the final analysis, he was not able to fulfill God's commission in his life. Quitting the commission God gave him, he sold the Lord for 30 pieces of silver and then hung himself. He began well, but he didn't endure.

Adolf Hitler began his career in a Catholic school and even wanted to be a priest. He began well, but then gave up to the demons of hell that sucked the world into a 12-year bloodbath called the Holocaust. Josef Stalin and Karl Marx both began as seminary students, but they missed the will of God in their life and dragged the world into the abyss of communism.

The Bible does not say that those shall be saved who began well. The Bible says that those who endure to the end shall be saved. Was there a time when you had a warm and wonderful relationship with the Lord? You began well, but the affairs of this life and the cares of this world have caused you to surrender the divine purpose for which God called you. You will never succeed, you will never have peace, you will never have joy, you will never have family unity, until you surrender to the purpose of Christ and persist to the end.

All great living begins when you look yourself in the face and refuse to allow yourself to play the role of a coward one more time. You make up your mind you're going to persevere, that you're going to endure, that you're going to stand in the winner's circle by God's grace. Not every race is won in the first lap. Not every ball game is won in the sixth inning or the third quarter. Not every marriage is wonderful all the time. Not every business makes a million dollars. Not every relationship ends in a friendship. Not every phone call results in a sale. Not every steak you eat is going to be tender. I ate a tough steak this week. I'm not going to go out and protest cows for the rest of my life. I'm going to try again.

Find God's purpose for your life

Perseverance is sustained by a God-given purpose. One of the great novels written in the 20th century was about the great depression in Ireland. No one had jobs. Men became drunkards, filled with depression. Their marriages were destroyed. Child abuse became rampant. Then the government created jobs on a large scale, to get everyone working again. A group of men began to build a road. They laughed and sang as they worked. Suddenly life had a purpose again. The singing and the laughter abruptly stopped when they discovered that the road they were building went nowhere. It simply ended in the middle of oblivion, an unnecessary road to nowhere. One by one they quit, because they had lost their purpose in life. And life without purpose is really a living death.

Some Christians never find God's purpose for their lives. I want you to understand that God is a God of purpose. Proverbs 19:21 says, "Many are the plans in a man's heart, but it is the Lord's purpose that prevails." That simply means that it makes no difference what you have planned, it's what God has planned for your life that's going to succeed.

Romans 8:28 says, "We know that all things work together for good to them that love God, to them who are the called according to his purpose." What is your divine purpose? If you have a purpose, then you can pursue it with a passion. But if you have no purpose, you will have no passion, and you will not persevere.

What is sin? In the Greek the word sin literally means "to miss the mark." Sin is not just committing adultery or robbing banks or beating up people. You sin simply by missing the mark of God in your life. If it's

God's purpose for you to sing in the choir, you're living in sin sitting in the pew. You're missing the purpose of God. If it's God's purpose for you to be a home minister and you'd rather play bridge on Thursday night, you're living in sin. You're missing the mark of God. The place of God's purpose is the place of God's power. Do you want God's power? Then get where God's purpose for your life happens to be. Surrender to it and pursue it.

God told Elijah to go to the house of the widow woman. "I'll feed you there," God said. "I'm not going to feed you somewhere, I'll feed you right there. You get one mile short or one mile on the other side, and you're going to starve to death. You get where I want you to be, and I'm going to pour out a blessing like Israel has never seen." And he went there and the widow woman prospered as the barrel of meal and cruse of oil were constantly refilled by the supernatural power of God. They were in the place of God's power because they were pursuing God's purpose.

Jesus said to the disciples, "Tarry in Jerusalem. Go to the upper room and I'll send the Holy Spirit there. I'm not going to send it to Antioch, I'm going to send it to the upper room. You go where I want you to be and when you are there, in the place of my purpose, I'll send my power." Some of you haven't felt God's power in years, because you don't have God's purpose. You're not tuned into God's plan and you have no perseverance at all.

Only God can show you the purpose for your life. Most of you have a warranty book in the glove compartment of your car. It says something like this, "Take this car only to an authorized dealer." If you take it to an unauthorized dealer, they won't honor the warranty. The authorized dealer is the one who made the car. Who knows Ford better than Ford? Who knows Toyota better than Toyota? If you take your Toyota to a Ford dealer, you're going to lose your warranty. Who made you? God. He is your "authorized dealer." So why are you running around and having your lives adjusted by the Norman Lears and the Hollywood set? And why are you having your minds adjusted by the secular humanists and the New Agers? They don't have the answer for your life. God is your maker. He knows the purpose for your life.

Who knows more about you, God who made you, or this intellectual riffraff out of Hollywood? God knows. The Bible is the manufacturer's manual for your soul. It is the manufacturer's manual for your marriage, your business, for your family relationships, for your health. Only God can give you the genuine spare parts for your life. If you're going to an unauthorized dealer, all you're going to have is a life filled with confusion and heartache. Go to the maker. Go to the living word of God. Discover your purpose, and then when you've found the purpose of God, pursue it with a holy passion. And persevere. Endure with a bulldog grit. Do not even begin to consider stopping short of the goal of God. Fight the good fight of faith and make up your mind you're going to win no matter what the cost. You are a child of God. The royal blood of heaven is flowing in your veins. Quitting is unthinkable.

Unless you pursue God's purposes with divine persistence, you'll never amount to the snap of your fingers. You may be talented. You may be educated. You may be full of dash and flash. But you're not worth the snap of your fingers if quitting is your middle name. Be persistent. Be more than a conqueror through Jesus Christ. Endure to the end.

Chapter 7
Success That Loves

Our lives are shaped by the people who love us and by those who refuse to love us.

Love is a mystery. One of the greatest mysteries in life is how the dumbbell who marries your daughter can be the father of the world's most brilliant grandchild just two years later.

What is love? Love is not the same as emotion. Love begins with an act of your will. But young people come into my office for counseling before marriage and they'll say things like, "I'm so in love. When I see him, I can't catch my breath and my face turns red." "That's not love, that's asthma," I tell them. Or, "I'm so in love. When I see her I can't think straight. My mind goes blank and I can't remember my name when I'm with her." "Perhaps you've confused love with amnesia," I say.

Why do we confuse emotion with love? Hollywood helped sell us that idea. It's even worse when Hollywood tries to talk about God's love. "Somebody up there likes me," you'll hear them say in the movies. Let's get something straight. Nobody up there likes you. No one in heaven — not God the Father, not Jesus Christ, not the Holy Spirit — nobody in heaven likes you. You like your car. You like your dog. You like your golf clubs. But God doesn't like you. He *loves* you.

"For God so loved the world, that he gave his only begotten Son, that whosoever believeth in him should not perish, but have everlasting life" (John 3:16). God does not love you because you deserve it. He does not love you because you've earned it. He does not love you because of your power or your possessions. God loves you because God *is* love. Love is his nature and he cannot restrain himself from loving you.

It is the very nature of God to love the unlovable. He loved you when you were unlovable. When you were covered with the stench of sin his heart was broken for you. In your despicable condition God loved you so much that he sent his only Son to die for you. Even if no one on the face of this earth loves you, rejoice and be glad because God loves you. And Jesus loves you and died to redeem you from the gutters of sin.

Love must be demonstrated

Love is something you do. God so loved the world that he gave his son. If you love your wife, you will find some way to express your love for her. You don't just tell her you love her, you show her your love. You do something to demonstrate that love.

Without love you are emotionally and spiritually dead. "We know that we have passed from death unto life, because we love the brethren. He that loveth not his brother abideth in death" (1 John 3:14). If you do not love the brethren, God says you are spiritually dead. Would you rather be where the world is or gathered with the righteous? Let me phrase that a little closer to home. Would you rather be around the children of God or at the Crystal Pistol with all the lounge lizards on Saturday night? "Beloved, let us love one another... for love is of God; and every one that loveth is born of God, and knoweth God" (1 John 4:7).

Emotion is not love, and sex is not love. There is a difference between love and lust. Love gives and lust takes. Sex is wonderful. It's God's idea. But it's for a man and a woman committed to each other in the covenant of matrimony. Young lady, if your date is a macho meathead who says something like, "If you really love me, let's go all the way," slap his face until his ears ring like cattle bells on a cold Christmas morning. If he asks you why, say, "My preacher told me to!" Sex is not the same thing as love.

Love is not to be confused with duty. I've heard men say, "I work hard and provide food, clothing and shelter for my family. That's proof that I love them." That's not showing your love, it's merely doing your duty. "If any provide not for his own, and specially for those of his own house, he hath denied the faith, and is worse than an infidel" (1 Tim. 5:8). Millions of fathers in America have left their families without support. Being a male is a matter of chance; being a man is a matter of choice. I call upon the prodigal fathers of America to do what God has asked of you: Do your duty and support your wife and children. Quit being a parasite on the taxpayers of America.

I watched a program on the Discovery Channel recently about a family of lions in Africa. The adult lion was making a den for the young cubs, showing them how to hunt for food, bathing them by licking with the tongue, showing approval when they did well. Even lions know how to do their duty and show affection. I thought how this wild animal was showing more compassion for its offspring than many fathers in America show to their children. Dads, do more for your children than just provide for them. If you want to spend something valuable on your children, spend time with them. Gifts are often the empty excuses of a delinquent parent. And the most important thing a father can do for his children is to love and respect their mother.

Don't confuse duty with love. Duty goes the first mile; love goes the extra mile. The old saying about going the extra mile (or the second mile) comes from the Bible. In the Sermon on the Mount Jesus said, "And whosoever shall compel thee to go a mile, go with him twain [two]" (Matt. 5:41). The Romans occupied Palestine in the days of Christ. Under their law, a Roman soldier could compel a Jewish man to carry his pack one mile. The Jews developed the custom of placing a marker, or milestone, one mile from the edge of their property. So if a Roman soldier came by and told him to carry his pack, the Jewish man would carry the pack as far as the milestone and then drop it promptly. He had grudgingly done his duty to the last inch. Jesus was telling his disciples, "Duty carries that pack the first mile; but love joyfully carries it the second mile." Love is not doing something for which you will receive something in return. Love is doing something even when you know you will never receive an equal reward.

Learn to accept yourself

Where does love begin? It begins with you. The Bible says to "love thy neighbor as thyself" (Lev. 19:18; Luke 10:27). If you don't like yourself, you won't like your neighbor. Most Americans, if given the chance, would like to be someone else. Some people complain about being too tall and skinny. (I think they're the lucky ones.) Others are so big they can get group insurance all by themselves. A woman asked her husband, "Will you love me when my hair turns gray?" He said, "Why not? I've loved you through five other shades." Americans not only love to change their hair color, we want the plastic surgeon to mold and shape our faces and our bodies until they look just the way we want. We're not satisfied with ourselves. But if you can't accept yourself the way you are, you can't accept anyone else and you can't love anyone else.

Long before the American Psychiatric Association came along, doctors came up with a way to describe personality types or temperaments. These temperaments were defined several hundred years before Christ. The four temperaments are sanguine, choleric, melancholy and phlegmatic. No one is made up 100% of one temperament, but you will be a strong mixture of one or two of the four temperaments. I want to take time to tell you a little about this because it will help you understand yourself and your family members, and help you accept and love yourself and others.

A sanguine temperament is warm and lively and loves to talk. Their feelings predominate in everything they do. They have an unusual capacity to enjoy themselves. They are great story tellers, never at a loss for words, and often speak without thinking. Sanguines often appear more confident than they really are. They make great salesmen, teachers, actors and speakers.

The apostle Peter was a sanguine. He was always the first to express his opinion and his feelings were always right on the surface. When Jesus told his disciples he would have to die, sanguine Peter said, "Oh no, you're not. We'll take up swords and fight for you." If he had stopped to think, he would have realized they would have had no chance against the Roman army. But that's just it — a sanguine rarely stops to think. Peter swore he was ready to die with Jesus and would never forsake him. Jesus said, "Peter, before this night is out you will deny me three times."

Impulsive Peter, who wanted to walk on the water while the others were content to sit in the boat, was the first to have a miracle ministry. Peter, whose loose tongue got him into trouble, was the one who preached the sermon on the Day of Pentecost when 3,000 people were saved. The point is that God knew the strengths and weaknesses of his personality. God took what he was and caused him to be effective in the ministry. God can use you where you are, just like you are, if you will quit hating what you are.

The apostle Paul was a choleric. He was strong-willed and hot-tempered. When the high priest instructed someone close to Paul to slap him, Paul looked him in the eye and said, "God will strike you, you hypocrite!" One time Paul was falsely arrested and placed in prison. If you put a Roman citizen in jail falsely, you could have your head cut off. When they found out that Paul was a Roman citizen as well as a Jew, they sent some junior official to set Paul free immediately. When the junior official came traipsing down the hall with the jail house key, Paul said, "Don't touch that lock. You go get the mayor, the city council, all three TV stations and both newspapers and then come down here and make a formal apology when you let me out."

Cholerics are quick, active, practical, independent, decisive and very opinionated. They thrive on making things happen. They take bold stands on issues and crusade against social injustice. They are not frightened by adversity, in fact, they enjoy a good fight. Cholerics are born leaders with dogged determination. Their weakness is that they don't analyze and details bore them. When they see a goal, they'll run over people in their rush to get there. They can be insufferably domineering. But they make great executives, generals and leaders, and, depending on their moral character, master criminals or dictators.

The apostle Thomas had a melancholy temperament. The melancholy person always sees the dark side of things. Thomas followed Jesus for three years. He saw all the miracles. He wasn't with the other disciples when they learned of Jesus' resurrection. He was probably walking the streets of Jerusalem, wringing his hands and saying, "We should have known you can't fight city hall. We were fools to give up our fishing business and follow an unemployed carpenter." When they told Thomas that Jesus was alive, he said, "I won't believe it unless I see it myself."

Melancholy people are moody and prone to depression. They are deeply analytical and critical of themselves. They are sensitive, perfectionistic and introverted, and quite often the most gifted and talented people around. They make wonderful artists, musicians, and inventors. But they often invite suffering and sadness to their lives.

The phlegmatic temperament is calm, cool and collected. It takes a lot to get a phlegmatic to the boiling point; they're slow to anger, consistent every time you see them, and avoid getting overly involved in things. A phlegmatic can tell a joke and never crack a smile. They feel more emotion than they show. They have little sympathy for the mood swings of the melancholy and enjoy throwing ice water all over the action-packed choleric. They love meticulous work and make great accountants and scientists.

Did you see yourself in the description of these four temperaments? Did you see your family members? I took the time to describe these personality types, because I want you to understand yourself better and to accept who you are. If you're always trying to be like somebody else, you'll never succeed. And you'll never love anyone else until you are comfortable with who God made you to be. God loves you, and he can use you. He knows your strengths and your weaknesses. Love God, love yourself, and love other people.

When I was a teenager, I worked at an orphanage in Houston, Texas. One morning when I arrived at work, I found a five-year-old boy dressed in a blue and white sailor suit, with his right hand tied to the fence post with a cotton rope. A note from his mother was pinned to his little sailor suit saying that she was not able to raise him. His little eyes brimmed with tears as I read that note. Full of bewilderment and uncertainty, he looked up at me and said, "Mister, what is your name?" I said, "My name is John Hagee." He said, "Mr. Hagee, would you hold me and hold me real tight?" I thought my heart would break as I wrapped my arms around that little tyke who had been abandoned by a hopeless mother.

I sometimes think of Robbie, that's what we came to

call that little boy, and I think how Robbie is the spitting image of so many Americans right now. We are a nation that has an abundance of everything but love. People of all ages and every social standing are waiting for someone to put their arms around them and hold them real tight until the fear goes away, until the hurt and the pain subside. This nation will never be a strong nation again if we don't start loving each other. I'm talking about loving the unlovable, those who don't have the same social and economic standing as you, those who don't have the education you have, those who can never give you back any thing at all. When you put your arms around people from whom you have no hope of any reciprocal gift, you give them the greatest gift of all — the gift of love.

Live each day as if it were your last

How is love sustained? By living each day as if it were your last. I have been preaching the gospel now for 34 years. I have officiated at hundreds of funerals over the years. I've stood beside so many caskets and heard the sobbing statements of farewell. I suppose I could write a novel from the things I've heard. Husbands say, "Honey, I wish we had taken that vacation we always talked about ... I wish we hadn't put off so many things until we retired, because you didn't make it to retirement with me ... I wish we had lived a little slower, loved a little deeper, stopped to smell the roses along the way." Wives say, "Honey, I'd trade all these possessions you worked so hard to get for just one more day with you ... just to hear your voice, just to hold you in my arms one more time."

How would you love and live if this were your last day on earth? Would you go upstairs and start World War III because he left his socks on the bedroom floor or she left the cap off the toothpaste? Would you leave for work without kissing your children and hugging them tight? Would you let your husband leave with angry words ringing in his ears over something so trivial it will soon be forgotten?

One of these days you're going to eat breakfast together for the last time. You're going to kiss each other good-bye for the last time. When you stand by that casket, will your mind be flooded with a sea of hateful things you wish you hadn't said? One of the saddest moments I have known as a pastor was spent listening to a sobbing husband tell about the horrible argument he had with his wife over absolutely nothing. She got in the car to go to the store to get milk and bread, and was killed before she got back home. Those painful moments of useless anger will haunt him the rest of his life.

Are you living and loving each day like it was your last day? Are you allowing the love of God to rule your heart and your home? You will never succeed until you learn to love with the love of God.

Blessing or Curses

Chapter 8
Curses: Their Cause and Cure

Is it possible that you or a member of your family could be living under the power of a curse? Perhaps you think that sounds superstitious and positively medieval. Believe me, curses are very real, and they have real power.

We are going to discover from God's word the reality of curses: the curse of God upon the ungodly, curses that are self-inflicted, curses that parents bring on their children, curses that follow a person, family or nation until they are supernaturally broken.

In the 30th chapter of Deuteronomy, Moses is giving his State of the Union address to Israel. It is the last time he will speak to them. And he makes this shocking statement: "I call heaven and earth to record this day against you, that I have set before you life and death, blessing and cursing: therefore choose life, that both thou and thy seed may live" (verse 19).

According to scripture, blessing is brought through obedience. A curse is brought by disobedience. It is what you do in relationship to what God has said that determines your blessing or your curse. In the text just referred to (Deut. 30:19), there are only two Bible positions in which you can live: under blessing or under a curse. The choice is yours.

You have seen people who were controlled by a curse. You probably didn't call it a curse; you may have called it a jinx. They are good people, people who are trying, but people who never reach their goal. They have talent, they have ability, they do all the right things, they read all the right books, they join the right organizations, and yet success always eludes them. Finally they say, "What's the use? Nothing ever goes right for me. My mother (father/sister/brother) has the same problem. I guess I'm just jinxed."

Has it ever seemed like an invisible hand reached out to grab you or members of your family just as you reach for the prize? It happens over and over and over. There is no logical explanation for it. The word that defines you is frustrated, because you never arrive at your goal. The pattern affects every area of your life — your business, your marriage, your health, your finances, but especially your relationships. Sometimes people living under a curse may have success, but they do not enjoy their success. Suddenly, and for no reason, they are dissatisfied, and depression settles over them like a black cloud. They say, "What's wrong with me? I should be enjoying life." But they do not.

I want you to hear this. There is hope. God has a remedy. For whom the Son sets free is free indeed. God has an answer for you.

I'm going to take great lengths to establish this, because, first of all, some of you have been taught in your theology classes that there's no such thing as a curse, and secondly, if there is such a thing, it could not happen to you. Understand that there's a difference between interpreting scripture and ignoring scripture. If you interpret all of scripture, you get one picture. But if you ignore a lot of scripture and only quote two verses, you can prove that only pink elephants are going to heaven.

The Genesis curses

The first and the best known curse is found in Genesis 3. When Adam and Eve sinned by partaking of the forbidden fruit, God spoke a curse into existence. He placed a curse upon the ground, saying thorns and thistles would grow. For that reason, until this very day, you can grow Johnson grass in the middle of 20 acres of asphalt when you can't grow wheat in the middle of a plowed field.

God placed a curse upon man. He said, "You will earn your living by the sweat of your brow." Welfare is against the plan of God. It was then and it is now. A man who does not work should not eat. Then there's a curse upon woman. God said, "Your sorrow shall be multiplied in conception and your desire shall be unto your husband." The Hebrew word translated desire does not mean sexual desire. It means that the woman's desire to rule in the home will be subordinated to the man's spiritual authority. The feminist movement is an open attack on God's spiritual authority for the home.

God also placed a curse upon the serpent. "You will crawl on your belly in the dirt for the rest of your days," God said. There is reason to believe that the serpent originally walked. The Hebrew word for his name in Genesis means "the shining one." But from that day until this, he has been the hated one, the ugly one who crawls in the dirt. The curse upon Satan also said that the seed of the woman would crush the head of the serpent. That happened at Calvary. When Jesus Christ, the seed of the woman, went to the cross of Calvary, he crushed the head of Satan. Satan is a liar, but Jesus is the way, the truth and the life. He came to break the curse of sin and Satan, to pull down the powers and the principalities of darkness.

If you think the Genesis curse is not real, find me a snake that doesn't crawl. Find a woman who has children without pain, or a man who earns his living without the sweat of his brow, or ground that won't grow thorns and thistles. Curses are very real.

A husband's death sentence on his wife

A second major curse in the Bible is found in Genesis 31. This story is about a husband who pronounced the death sentence on his wife. As Jacob and his wives and children prepare to return to Canaan, Rachel steals her father Laban's idols or "household gods." She wanted these good luck charms. Laban comes chasing after them and Jacob, not knowing that his wife had stolen the idols, said "With whomsoever thou findest thy gods, let him not live" (verse 32). It was a curse of death. Did it happen? Yes. Genesis 35:16 says Rachel died in childbirth, while in the prime of her life, according to the curse placed on her by her husband.

The point is this: Father, you are the spiritual authority in your home. Be careful what you say about your wife. Be careful what you say about your children or to your children. The Bible says that the power of life and death is in the tongue (Prov. 18:21). You curse your son or your daughter when you say something like, "you're dumb," or "you're stupid." You have just spoken a curse over you daughter or son. In effect, you're saying, "You don't have the ability learn. You will be a remedial student. You will be insecure and a guaranteed failure from this day forward because of my toxic mouth." When you say, "You'll never amount to anything," you have just cursed your child's ability to succeed. You have just destroyed their financial future and their ability to earn a living for their family. Life and death are in the power of the tongue.

Words have power. Words have life. They can destroy. Wounds that are inflicted by a sword quickly heal. But wounds inflicted by words produce a cancer of the soul that destroys for generations to come. "Death and life are in the power of the tongue" (Prov. 18:21). "A wholesome tongue is a tree of life" (Prov. 15:4). "A hypocrite with his mouth destroyeth his neighbor: but through knowledge shall the just be delivered" (Prov. 11:9). "The tongue is a fire, a world of iniquity ... and it is set on fire of hell" (James 3:6).

The Bible plainly teaches that you can murder someone with your speech just as surely as you can murder them with a .44 magnum pistol. The ability to speak is a God-given ability, designed so that you may praise the Lord. But you can take your tongue and murder someone's character, destroy their good works and assassinate their ministry. God calls you an accuser of the brethren, and you will one day stand before God and give an answer for every word you have ever uttered.

The Jericho curse

The third major curse in the Bible is the curse upon the city of Jericho. When Israel defeated Jericho, Joshua pronounced a curse upon the city that continues until this day. "Cursed be the man before the Lord, that riseth up and buildeth this city Jericho: he shall lay the foundation thereof in his first-born, and in his youngest son shall he set up the gates of it" (Joshua 6:26). Simply stated, if man tries to rebuild Jericho, his oldest son will die when he starts, and should he stay with it long enough to put up the gates, his youngest son will die. Did that ever happen? Yes. Hundreds of years later, during the administration of Ahab, a man by the name of Hiel tried to rebuild the city of Jericho. 1 Kings 16:34 says that his oldest and youngest sons died exactly according to the curse spoken by Joshua.

On one of my trips to Israel our tour guide told us that 30 years ago a man started to rebuild Jericho as a tourist attraction. When he started, his oldest son died suddenly and unexpectedly. He stopped building. I can assure you that if he had continued, his youngest son would have died, because curses follow you from generation to generation until they are bound and broken in the name and authority of Jesus Christ.

Scriptural reasons for curses

Every curse has a cause. Proverbs 26:2 says that an undeserved curse will not come to rest. When someone speaks a curse, if you have a deficiency in your life, it will stick. But if you are covered by the blood of Jesus, it cannot. If you come under a curse, you need to examine why.

Here are some Bible reasons that curses exist in the lives of people. First, a father can place a curse on his family by participating in crooked business deals. Proverbs 17:13 says, "Whoso rewardeth evil for good, evil shall not depart from his house." If a father returns evil for good, evil will stalk his children all the days of their life. In American history there have been several very rich and powerful tycoons who made their fortunes grinding the face of the poor. Their children grew up to have fame and power, but they lived in shame and tragedy that followed them doggedly all their days. If you, father, participate in crooked business deals and grind the face of the poor to gain your wealth, the judgment of God will be upon you and your children and your children's children.

There is also a curse for recognizing false gods. "Thou shalt have no other gods before me" (Exod. 20:3). That's the first of the ten commandments, and most people can quote that. But stay tuned. "Thou shalt not make unto thee any graven image [that's a statue], or any likeness of any thing that is in heaven above, or that is in the earth beneath ... for I the Lord thy God am a jealous God, visiting the iniquity of the fathers upon the children unto the third and fourth generation of them that hate me" (Exod. 20:4-5). Four generations — that's 160 years. God says if you have in your home a statue of any other god, you hate me. That's strong. Jesus said the same thing. He said if you're not for me, you're against me. You cannot be on both sides of this issue.

Father, mother, if you want to bring the curse of God to your children for four generations, fill your home with statues of any god. Put that statue on the dashboard of your car or on your charm bracelet or around your neck, and you are living in what the Bible calls spiritual adultery. It brings the wrath of God permanently, until it's repented of and broken in the supernatural. There was a woman in my church years ago whose life was a living nightmare. Everything she put her hand to collapsed. She thought she was jinxed. Those were her words. She asked me to come to her house and talk to her. I went to her house; it was filled with statues of dragons. The Bible says that Satan is "that old dragon, the devil." I said, "Lady, it is my belief that if you recognize Satan in any way — with statues, with the occult, with witchcraft, with Ouija boards, with mind control, with Eastern philosophies — then Satan has a legal right for his demon powers to live in your house. He has a legal right to claim your life, your soul and your children. She threw those dragons out and her life turned around immediately, permanently and for the good, because she obeyed the Lord.

It is not enough to recognize God as the first and greatest god. You must recognize him as the only God. Isaiah 45:21 says, "There is no God else beside me ... there is none beside me." Jesus cannot be placed on the mantle with other gods. He is either Lord of all, or he's not Lord at all.

Is God the Father your only god? Not if you're into the New Age, he's not. Not if you're into witchcraft. Not if you're into Satanism. Not if you're into humanism. Is Jesus Christ the only Lord of your life? Not if you're dominated by the world, the flesh and the devil. And if he's not the Lord of your life, the judgment of God is upon you and will follow you like an invisible hand until you serve the Lord with all of your heart, soul, mind and body.

Anti-semitism brings the curse of God. Anti-semitism is hatred toward the Jewish people. God said to Abraham, the father of the Jewish people, "This is my foreign policy concerning Israel and the Jewish people: I will bless those who bless you and I will curse those who curse you. And through you shall the nations of the world be blessed" (Gen. 12:3).

It's a historical fact that the nations of the world have been blessed through the Jewish people. Jesus said that "salvation is of the Jews" (John 4:22). It was the Jewish people that gave us the patriarchs, Abraham, Isaac and Jacob. It was the Jewish people that gave us the prophets — Daniel, Ezekiel, Jeremiah, Isaiah — there's not a Baptist in the bunch. Mary and Joseph — the Jewish family into which our Lord and Savior Jesus Christ was born. Mary and Joseph were not known as Mr. and Mrs. Christ, One Cave Lane, Bethlehem, Palestine. They were Mr. and Mrs. Rabinowitz, or Mr. and Mrs. Goldberg. Almost all of the Bible was written by Jewish people. I believe that's why Satan hates the Jewish people so intently: They produced the word of God and they produced the Son of God that broke Satan's hold over humanity. Anti-Semitism is a demonic spirit born in the bowels of hell to retaliate against the Jewish people for the good things they have done to bring the light of God to humanity.

Many of the medical discoveries that have saved millions of lives are the product of the brilliance of Jewish minds. They have given us scientists and statesmen and master merchants and scholars and musicians. Few Americans know the role the Jewish people played in the American revolution. The Continental army was naked and hungry and shivering in the snows of Valley Forge. They were discouraged and desperate for arms and ammunition. Hiam Solomon, a Jewish Philadelphia banker, arranged a loan of several million dollars, without interest. The additional funds turned the tide in the war for independence. George Washington, the father of our country, was so appreciative of what Hiam Solomon did that he placed a tribute to the Jewish people on the back of the dollar bill that you carry in your pocket to this day. Over the head of the eagle is the cloudburst of the shekinah glory of God, and inside that is the Mogen David, the six-pointed Star of David. Turning the eagle upside down, you see the menorah. The design of the dollar bill is a tribute to the Jewish people and their contribution to freedom in America.

Church, it is time for Christians to stop praising the dead Jews of the past, Abraham, Isaac and Jacob, while hating the Jews across the street. They are the seed of Abraham. God loves them and they are the apple of his eye and they are the family of God. Whatever you do to the Jewish people, God will do to you. If you bless them, God will bless you. And if you curse them, the judgment of God will come upon you.

Let me validate that scripturally and historically. Hamaan, the Old Testament Hitler, plotted to have the Jews of Persia, which is modern Iran, exterminated. At this point in history, most of the Jewish people were living in Persia. Had he been successful, the word of God would never have been published. And Jesus Christ would never have been born. Hamaan built a gallows upon which to hang the Jews. But when the story ends, he and his sons were hung on the gallows he planned for the Jewish people. "I will curse those who curse you."

In 1933 Adolf Hitler raised his hand and was sworn in as the chancellor of Germany. His goose-stepping, demonized, Nazi legions began to systematically destroy six million Jewish people. These Nazi officials were baptized Christians, in good standing with the church of Rome, who were not then, or at any time since, condemned for their heinous crimes against the Jewish people. But there is going to come a judgment day. And Adolf Hitler and his high command will bow before a Jewish rabbi, Jesus Christ of Nazareth. They will weep and wail and grind their teeth. The bullies of Europe will tremble before the lion of the tribe of Judah and they will be sentenced to an everlasting hell where they will burn with fire forever.

Several years ago I was in West Berlin for a speaking engagement. This was before the Berlin wall came down, and we stood at Checkpoint Charlie with some Christians. One lady asked me "Pastor Hagee, why did God allow the communists to build a wall around us?" The answer I gave her was scriptural. "Because your fathers built a wall around the Jews at Auschwitz and Dachau and Bergenbelsen and other places," I said. I pointed out that the concentration camp at Dachau with its walls and gun towers is strikingly similar to the Berlin Wall. I continued, "Here is a fence 12 feet high with a no man's land, and a second fence that's electrified. That's how the Nazis built Dachau. You put machine gun towers down the middle, so have the communists. The Nazis put attack dogs down the middle, trained to kill. So have the communists. God has paid you back down to the dog hair."

Israel is the only nation created by a sovereign act of God. The title deed to the nation of Israel is recorded in the book of Genesis. All other nations were created by an act of men, but Israel was created by God. God defends Israel. "He that keepeth [a military term] Israel shall neither slumber nor sleep" (Psalm 121:4). Now if God created Israel, if God loves Israel and defends Israel, does it not make sense to say that those who fight with Israel are fighting against God Almighty? I want to say this to the U. S. State Department in this new administration: *Bless Israel.* Do not afflict the nation of Israel, because God is on the side of Israel.

Self-inflicted curses

Finally, there are curses you bring on yourself. "Cursed is the man who dishonors his father or his mother" (Deut. 27:16). Let me tell you emphatically that millions of America's young people are under the curse of God for their rebellion against their mothers and fathers. The Bible says, "Honor thy father and mother ... that it may be well with thee, and thou mayest live long on the earth" (Eph. 6:2-3). If you dishonor your parents, if you rebel against them, it will not be well with you and you will not live long. You'll have a short life, full of trouble, that will end prematurely. God is a father and he demands obedience. If you do not obey your earthly parents, he will have the last word with you.

"Cursed is the man who withholds justice from the alien, the fatherless or the widow" (Deut. 27:19). An alien is a person without citizenship. Today, in this part of America, that would apply to Mexican aliens. Simply stated, if you employ a maid in your home who is a Mexican alien, and you work her like a slave and do not pay her a fair wage, the curse of God is upon you. When you bring her into your home, treat her like a human being and pay her a fair wage, or you will answer to God Almighty. Let me add a footnote. If you don't pay her social security taxes, you can't be Attorney General! (I just couldn't pass that up.)

"Cursed is the man who sleeps with his father's

wife" (Deut. 27:20). "No one is to approach any close relative to have sexual relations" (Lev. 18:6). Incest brings the curse of God. Fathers, if you are sexually abusing your daughter, you may have your wife intimidated, and you may have your daughter terrorized, but you don't have God terrorized — and the judgment of God is right behind you. The only reason he hasn't smashed you like a peanut under the hoof of an elephant is because of his mercy. Do not overstep the bounds of God's mercy, because God will take you out if you continue to torment your daughter.

"This is the curse that goeth forth over the face of whole earth: for everyone that stealeth shall be cut off" (Zech. 5:3). Do you steal from your employer? God will cut you off. You're under a curse. Do you steal from department stores? God will cut you off. When you see the riots in L. A., or wherever they happen to be taking place, I want you to know that every one who robs and loots is under the curse of God. Until you take what you stole back or make remuneration for it, the judgment of God is going to follow you and your children for 160 years. It's not worth it. Take it back today.

There is a financial curse in Malachi 3:8-9. The word of God says, "Will a man rob God? Yet ye have robbed me. But ye say, Wherein have we robbed thee? In tithes and offerings. Ye are cursed with a curse: for ye have robbed me, even this whole nation." Tithing is step one to financial independence. When you tithe God blesses you because of your obedience to his word. When you refuse to tithe, God cuts you and calls you a thief. He has your mug shot on his bulletin board in heaven. Some of you came to church this morning driving stolen cars, wearing stolen clothes and stolen jewelry. You took God's money and bought those things. Let me tell you something: God plays hardball. God doesn't sit up in heaven saying, "Oh my, they're not obeying me. What'll I do?" God controls your breath. He controls your heartbeat. God says "Hey, I can get his attention." Then he shuts off your business. He sees to it that your new car breaks down, once a week. He has your mother-in-law move in with you. He has the IRS call and say they're auditing you all the way back to the Civil War. He puts you in the Baptist hospital with your feet in a body cast and your arms stretched towards the heavens and cables pulling you in all four directions. You say, "I wonder if God is trying to speak to me?" Yes, Bubba, he is!

What happens when you tithe? "Prove me now herewith, saith the Lord of hosts, if I will not open you the windows of heaven, and pour you out a blessing, that there shall not be room enough to receive it" (Malachi 3:10). Would you like a blessing from the Lord that you don't have the ability to contain? The answer is found in tithing. If you refuse to tithe, your business will just continue to decline. What do you have to lose, except your poverty?

"I have set before you life and death, blessing and cursing." It's your choice. Your decision to obey or disobey is what brings the blessing or the judgment of God. Choose blessing.

Chapter 9

America Under Curse

This week USA Today featured on the front page a picture of five young men carrying high-powered rifles and pistols. They have threatened to burn L. A. down if the verdict in the Rodney King case does not suit them. Where do these young people come from, these pistol-packing hoodlums who demand that the legal system in America mind them?

Where do they come from? They come from our public schools, where secular humanism has taught them there is no such thing as right or wrong. Where they have learned there are no moral absolutes, therefore just do whatever you want. Do your own thing. If it feels good, do it. If you want it, steal it. If someone resists you, shoot them.

They come from schools where they got grades they didn't work for, from teachers who are afraid of being assaulted in a blackboard jungle ruled by guns and knives and fear. The police chief said there are at least 100,000 gang members prepared to loot and destroy. These are America's new young barbarians. This is the generation of the future.

These barbarians come from schools where the ten commandments have been ripped off the wall by order of the Supreme Court, lest they have "a moral influence" on the students who might read them. Certainly America doesn't need moral influence — not in a nation where a woman is raped every 48 seconds ... where 25% of teenage girls live in constant fear of sexual assault from a relative ... where 80,000 people every year are shot in cold blood. Certainly we have no need for any moral instruction in our schools.

They come from schools where God and the Bible are politically incorrect ... from schools where condoms are passed out and "safe sex" is preached. A silly slogan promoting condom use is now the hope of a nation swimming in a moral sewer of AIDS and homosexuality and pornography. Ladies and gentlemen, the gospel of condoms and safe sex will not save America. The only gospel that will save America is the gospel of Jesus Christ our Lord and our Savior. St. Paul said, "I am not ashamed of the gospel of Christ: for it is the power of God unto salvation to every one that believeth" (Romans 1:16). This is a call to repentance and righteousness. It is not a call to rebellion and anarchy. This is a call to holiness, without which no man shall see the Lord. This is a call to sexual abstinence. What's wrong with morality? What's wrong with purity?

These new barbarians come from theaters where macho violence is romanticized and witchcraft is portrayed as the source of power ... where Jesus Christ is presented in such movies as *The Last Temptation of Christ* as a demonized, lust-driven, spineless, confused buffoon who doesn't know who he is and has to use Judas Iscariot as his personal counselor to find his way out of the fog. Hollywood hates God and hates Christianity.

Hollywood hates traditional family values. Hollywood is not a place; Hollywood is an industry whose celluloid sewage is a cancer on the soul of America.

Let me prove my point. Some 25,000 Christians gathered in front of Universal Studios to protest *The Last Temptation of Christ*. The movie moguls of America and their media stooges categorized these Bible-carrying demonstrators as "the lunatic fringe of religious fanatics, right-wing extremists." The Detroit *Free Press* called them "the American ignoramus faction, fun-loathing people full of self-righteous bile." Such objectivity makes you really love the media, doesn't it?

Compare that to the animal rights activists who demanded that Disney Studios eliminate one scene from a movie they considered to be "anti-wolf." They said that in the movie *White Fang,* a wolf attacked a man unprovoked, and they believed there was no scientific proof that a wolf will do that. The movie industry immediately took the offending scene out. The message? It's okay to be anti-Christ, but not anti-wolf.

In the movie *Cape Fear,* the vicious rapist-murderer is a Pentecostal Christian. He has tattoos of the cross on his body, and scripture verses on his arm. As he rapes his victims, he asks them, "Are you ready to be born again and speak in tongues?" If Hollywood did that to any minority group in America, they would be swimming in lawsuits and probably scraping up the ashes of what was left of their burned-out studios. But Christian bashing has become an art form in Hollywood.

What should we do? Ladies and gentlemen of America, there are 40 million of us who claim to believe the Bible as the source of truth. Stop attending any movie that attacks our faith. Stop giving your money to these media moguls who attack God, who attack family values and are re-writing American history. Enough is enough. I believe that if we march together, and pray together, we can drive them into bankruptcy, which is exactly where they ought to be.

These young pistol-packing gangsters come from rock concerts where rap music encourages them to shoot policemen in songs like *Cop Killer*. A boy heard it and went out and murdered a policeman in cold blood. Times Warner, who produced the song, has been sued and I hope they are sued out of business for putting out that kind of trash. Rock music promotes drug abuse, Satanism, rape, murder and suicide — they sing about it and then go out and do it.

These gangsters come from churches where they have stopped preaching the word of God and where Jesus Christ is no longer Lord ... where they have adopted a social action gospel ... where they have become addicted to a pop psychology. They have hype without holiness. They have abandoned righteousness for ritual. They have ordained homosexuals presenting the truth of God's word. What a cowardly abdication from the principles of truth.

They come from homes where the father is gone. Even in homes where the father is present, the majority of them are so preoccupied with the pursuit of power, profits and pleasure that they spend only seconds a day talking to their children.

They come from homes where the children sit in front of the television for 48 hours a week. The television set has becomes the national baby-sitter, brain-washing our children with violence, lust, greed, witchcraft and fear. A parent will say to me, "My children can't sleep at night." I say, "What are they watching on TV?" They're usually watching horror shows. Fear is a spirit and your child can get it from watching the television. You need to be the steward and the watchdog over your children. It is not a matter of censorship, it is a matter of living a godly and a holy life. If what's on the television does not glorify God and promote purity and holiness, then turn it off! You have no business watching it.

Signs of a nation under the curse of God

The judgment of God is not coming to America, it's here. Moses presents in Deuteronomy 28 the signs that a nation is under the curse of God. Remember that the basis of blessing is obedience. So the question must be asked: Has America been obedient to God? The answer is obviously no. America's number one problem is not the economy. America's number one problem is God, because God hates sin. He always judges sin, and America is saturated with sin. If God does not judge America, he will have to apologize to Sodom and Gomorrah. In truth, it would be proper for America to change our national symbol from an eagle to a buzzard. I used to say that society was going to the dogs. I no longer say that out of respect for dogs.

Consider the curse upon our cities. Moses wrote in Deut. 28:16, "Cursed shalt thou be in the city." And how is it in the cities of America? Gangs rule the streets with guns. The jails are flooded. Murderers and rapists are turned loose on the streets, on early parole, and they roam the streets like packs of wolves looking for new prey. When a criminal can hit you in the head with a pipe and he gets out of jail before you get out of the hospital, it's wrong. It's time for that to change. But it will not change, ladies and gentlemen, until you and you and you and you get a belly full and say, "Enough is enough. We want these rapists and murderers and criminals off the streets. Put them in jail and throw away the key."

How is it in the land of the free and the home of the brave? Here's how it is. We live behind doors locked with a series of dead bolts down the side. Every home must have a burglar alarm if you want to sell it to someone. Our guns are cocked and loaded. Attack dogs are straining at the end of the leash, trained to kill. Ladies carry mace, just in case. I was going to the mall the other day and my mind was a million miles away. It was broad daylight. I wasn't even aware that I was about 10 feet behind a woman. She thought I was trailing her. All of a sudden she turns around, whips a whistle in her mouth and pulls out a can of mace. I threw my hands up and said, "Peace!" I almost made the 5:00 news.

How is it in our cities? Our home windows have bars over them like a penitentiary. We, the tax-paying citizens of America, are prisoners in our own homes. And now, even while locked in our houses, we are victims of drive-by shootings, random violence which is nothing more than recreational murder.

Consider the curse upon our economy. "Cursed shall be thy basket and thy store" (Deut. 28:17). "Basket and store" refer to the economy. So how is America's economy? We are 4.4 trillion dollars in debt, and that national debt is racing out of sight at the rate of 1 billion dollars a day. Last year it required all the taxes the IRS could collect from every citizen west of the Mississippi just to pay the interest on the national debt. The federal debt per person is now $18,000 for every man, woman, boy and girl. "But," you say, "the president has raised our taxes so that we can pay the national debt." The J. Peter Grace Commission released a study showing how

America spends its money. They found out that for every one dollar in new taxes, the federal government winds up spending a dollar and eighty cents. That means they only dig the ditch deeper. The fact is, our government is guilty of embezzlement from the social security fund. We have borrowed billions of dollars from the social security fund and replaced it with IOUs, pure paper. There is no money there. No one knows how to put it back. One of the solutions being offered is to raise the retirement age to 70. Another solution is to demand that all who are entitled to social security and who have enough money to live forfeit the money they have paid into the social security fund. You have to smoke marijuana — and inhale — to like either one of those solutions.

Banks in America will soon take a dive in a new wave of bank closures. The crisis will cost you, the taxpaying people of America, billions of dollars. A pension crisis is coming, created by industries investing retirement funds in junk bonds that are now worthless. It will make the S & L crisis mere child's play. Economists say we are racing toward a bankruptcy that will place our children and our grandchildren in an economic slavery to foreign countries. Blindly America is moving toward becoming a third world nation. There will be no recovery, simply because we have spent beyond our means for 40 years.

The president of the U.S. is soon going to be faced with two options. One, he can declare that America is actuarially bankrupt; or, two, he will instruct the treasury department to print more money, running the presses day and night, creating massive inflation in these United States. In the history of the world no nation who has found itself in the same debt posture as

America presently finds itself has ever escaped hyperinflation. Hyperinflation is coming. Get ready for it.

Next, consider the curse of incurable plagues. Moses writes in Deuteronomy 28:21-27 about pestilence, meaning sickness, and incurable diseases. AIDS is an incurable plague. Here is a medical fact you had better not forget: Everyone who gets AIDS dies. They can slow it down, but they can't cure it. There are thousands of silent carriers of this politically correct disease right now in America. There are differing opinions in the medical profession about how easy it is to get or how impossible it is to get. They do know that it costs $150,000 per year to treat one patient. And that's something else you taxpayers will be able to pay for when homosexuals invade the military and take it over. It's called the high cost of low living, and America's about to find out what that cost really is.

Then there is the curse of enemies defeating your armies. "The Lord shall cause thee to be smitten before thine enemies: thou shalt go out one way against them, and flee seven ways before them" (Deut. 28:25). Remember that Israel lost the battle to Ai because of sin in Israel. Sin is something God weighs and destroys a nation for. Weak enemies are defeating America. We lost in Korea. We lost in Vietnam. The sight of the American ambassador running for his helicopter with the flag folded under his arm, running from a nation the size of Vermont, defeated and humiliated, is a picture that is burned in the minds of Americans. I believe the American government owes an apology to every American soldier they sent into battle in Vietnam, where victory was not our goal and was not even possible. We owe them an apology.

What about Desert Storm? What you saw in Desert Storm was triumph without victory. It was the New World Order on parade. But Saddam Hussein is still in power. He still has nuclear capability. He still hates Israel, and he still intends to conquer Jerusalem. What really happened in Desert Storm? Number one, Israel was attacked, and God says that when it comes to keeping watch over Israel, he neither slumbers nor sleeps (Psalm 121). Second, the report has come to us from our spirit-filled chaplains there about unusual weather conditions they believe were divinely ordained. Americans were worried about mine fields and the possibility of losing thousands of soldiers in the first two weeks of a ground war. But the night before the invasion an unexpected rain storm washed the sand off the mines, exposing them in plain sight. Our troops went out, clipped the wires, and raced on to the battle front. That's the hand of God.

America has not been a winner in major warfare since World War II. One whole generation has known nothing but defeat and humiliation at the hand of our enemies. And that is the sign of a nation under the judgment of God.

Consider the curse of divorce. Moses said, "Thou shalt betroth a wife, and another man shall lie with her: thou shalt build a house, and thou shall not dwell therein" (Deut. 28:30). Marriages are failing in America in record numbers. The traditional family in America is under attack by feminists, who say that marriage is slavery, and by social reconstructionists who want to redefine the family so that homosexuals can be legally married and adopt children. When the family falls, the church will fall and America will fall. The future of America is not going to be determined by politicians in

Washington. The future of America is going to be determined by godly parents teaching their children the precepts of the word of God, teaching them righteousness, truth and integrity.

Consider the curse upon our children. Moses says, "Thou shalt beget sons and daughters, but thou shalt not enjoy them; for they shall go into captivity" (Deut. 28:41). Do Americans enjoy their children? No. Over 4,000 of them are murdered every day in America's abortion mills. *Home Alone* is not just a movie, it's a national tragedy. Child abuse is a national shame. Child pornography so vile that I can't describe it is a multi-billion dollar industry in this nation. Pornography turns lust-driven men into animals who rape without conscience. I want to ask every father, how in the name of God can you take your money, walk into a pornography shop, and buy the trash that puts money in the hands of men who print materials that will inspire other men to rape your wife or daughter? How can you do that? You cannot do it in good conscience. I challenge you in the name of Jesus Christ to get that pornography out of your house. Throw it away. It's not art, it's trash.

Do we enjoy our children? No. We see the pictures of missing children on our milk cartons every morning to remind us we do not enjoy our children. If you escape the abortionist's knife as a child and you're born, then there's the drug pusher, and then there's the mad gunman at the mall, and the rapist at the park and the Satanists who are recruiting in the public schools, and some of them recruiting for human sacrifices. Police sources say that 2,000 children every year disappear, children who are too young to wander off by themselves. What happens to them?

Consider the curse of other nations who prosper at

our expense. Deuteronomy 28:43 says, "The stranger [foreigner] that is within thee shall get up above thee very high; and thou shalt come down very low." Foreigners are buying America out from under our feet. Buying the land, buying the businesses, buying the real estate, buying the industry. I'm not blaming the foreigners, but I ask you, whose financial interests are they going to have when an international financial crunch comes? It will not be yours, ladies and gentlemen of America.

Analysts tell us that economic time bombs have been planted on Wall Street. Foreign nations have invested heavily in stocks and bonds and now they say, "If your Congress does not vote the way we want, we will take our investments out overnight and send your economy plunging to the bottom." Did it ever dawn on you that we may not be in control of America's economic destiny any more? If we fail to do what other nations want, they will pull the plug and we will expire economically.

What is the solution? The solution does not rest with the President or with Congress. The solution does not rest with the world. The solution rests with the church of Jesus Christ. The Bible says in 2 Chronicles 7:14, "If my people, which are called by my name, shall humble themselves, and pray, and seek my face, and turn from their wicked ways; then will I hear from heaven, and will forgive their sin, and will heal their land." God begins by saying, "If my people, the people who are called by my name, will begin to pray and seek my face, I'll supernaturally do marvelous and wonderful things."

A call to take America back

So I'm saying to you, church of Jesus Christ in America, this is a call to righteousness and repentance. This is a call to a return to absolute loyalty to the word of God. What does absolute loyalty mean? It means that if the president calls for homosexuals to be in the military, we stand with the word of God that says homosexuality is an abomination unto God. If means that if Hillary Rodham Clinton calls for children to have the right to sue their parents, we stand with the word of God that requires children to honor their parents so that their days may be long upon the earth. It means that if the welfare department continues to tax men who will work and give the money to men who can work but won't work, we stand with the word of God that says the man who does not work shall not eat.

If it's politically incorrect to honor God, then we're politically incorrect and proud of it. In an America where the public schools have mocked God and thrown the Bible out, we lift our voices today, and every day until Jesus Christ comes, to say that God is not mocked. "Know ye that the Lord he is God: it is he that hath made us, and not we ourselves" (Ps. 100:3).

This is a call for the church to defend the sanctity of life, to recognize "that all men are created equal, that they are endowed by their Creator with certain unalienable rights, that among these are *life* ..." We say no to abortion now — no today, no tomorrow, and no forever. We will never accept it.

We affirm that in the beginning God created Adam and Eve, not Adam and Bruce. God intended for marriage to be between one man and one woman for life. Homosexuality is an abomination to God, and it will always be an abomination to God. It is a choice of lifestyle, a learned behavior, and there is hope for the homosexual who wants to be set free by the power of Jesus Christ.

We affirm that the family plan is God's plan. In spite of the assault on the traditional family, in spite of the attack on marriage and motherhood, the family will endure forever, because it's God's plan. Children are the heritage of the Lord. Therefore, the righteous in this church today demand that the pornography industry and the homosexual community and the drug pushers of America leave our children alone. They belong to us and we enjoy them as a blessing of God.

In closing, we affirm that the church of Jesus Christ is not a retirement center for spiritual fat cats. It is the recruiting center for the army of the Lord Jesus Christ. We are here to afflict the comforted and comfort the afflicted. We ask God Almighty to forgive us for sitting on the sidelines while hell's legions took America by storm. Now, saints of God around America who name Jesus as Lord and believe in this sacred text, let's take America back. We announce to the powers and the principalities in the heavens that we are no longer walking around in circles worrying about where hell's legions are going to attack next. With faith in God, with faith in his word, with faith in the blood of Jesus, we are going to charge the gates of hell until the victory is ours.

Christians of America, enough is enough. Let us arise and do exploits in the name of God. Let us reject the curse and receive the blessing. Let God arise and his enemies be scattered, in Jesus' name.

Chapter 10

The Blessing: Power and Purpose

Would you like to be supernaturally blessed in your finances, in your health, in your relationships, in your emotions, to be filled with peace that surpasses understanding, to have joy that's unspeakable and full of glory, and to have victory over the world, the flesh and the devil? The secret is in the supernatural power of the blessing. I want to share with you today a Bible mystery that has been lost to the Christian church for 2,000 years. It is a mystery the Jewish people have practiced from the time of Abraham, but it is something that we as a church have forgotten.

What are you really saying when you say, "God bless you?" When someone sneezes, we say, "Bless you." We have said it so often we no longer know what it actually means. There's an Irish blessing that goes, "May you be in heaven 30 minutes before the devil knows you're dead."

When you say, "I bless you in the name of the Lord," you're saying far more than you know. God instructed Moses to bless the children of Israel, saying,"The Lord bless you and keep you" (Numbers 6:24). It is God's will to bless you, not because you deserve it, but because it is the nature of God to bless. God does not love you, nor does God bless you, because of what you do. That's legalism, and you must be free from that. You cannot earn God's favor. God blesses you because he has chosen to bless you. He loves you because God is love, and it is his nature to love you.

What is a blessing? A blessing is the impartation of the supernatural power of God into a human life by the spoken word of God's delegated authority. Words have life and they have power. And when you begin to speak them as the spiritual authority, you can literally shape the destiny of a person's life. God told Moses, "This is how you are to bless the children of Israel. I want you to go and to tell them these exact words. And the moment you speak the words through Aaron, then the power of God will be released to every person in the tribe of Israel."

So I'm saying this today to every father: You are the spiritual authority in your home. With your spoken blessing over your children you can literally control their destiny and shape their future. The power of the blessing and the purpose of the blessing is to take charge of the destiny of the lives of your children. The moment you begin to speak a blessing over them, you release the protection of God into their life. You release prosperity. You release health. You release the anointing. You release the angels of God to guard them. You release the direction of God in their life. You take charge physically, spiritually and emotionally in their relationships, and you ought to do that today.

On the other hand, there are millions of America's children who are cursed by the toxic tongues of their parents. What comes out of the mouth of that father or mother has literally cursed that child's future. Father, when you say something like, "You're dumb," you have just cursed your child's ability to learn. When you say, "You never do anything right," you have just murdered their self-esteem. When you say, "You'll never amount to anything," you have just executed their financial future. Today I'm challenging you, as the spiritual head of your family, to take this principle and bless your children — not once a year, but every day of the world. When they get out of bed in the morning, put your hands on their heads and bless them for the day. They'll leave your house feeling like they could wrestle Hulk Hogan and win.

The history of the blessing

Let me give you a brief Bible history of the blessing. The first thing God did after he created Adam and Eve was to bless them. Then he gave them three commands. The first command was to "be fruitful and multiply." Some of you have taken that command more seriously than others. But abortion is rejection of the command to be fruitful and multiply. The second command was to "subdue" the earth. That's spiritual warfare. Spiritual warfare did not begin a few years ago when the charismatic movement started writing books about it. Spiritual warfare began in the book of Genesis, and it still rages. And it will not be over until the trump of God sounds. America is in a supernatural war for its very soul, and to the winner goes the prize of our children. We are either going to be the victors or the victims, and you might as well make up your mind to participate in the race, because the fight involves you and every member of your family.

Then the third command was to "take dominion." The idea that the church is not to be involved in the political process is a lie from hell. The Bible says that "when the righteous are in authority, the people rejoice: but when the wicked beareth rule, the people mourn" (Prov. 29:2). How can the righteous be in authority if they don't get involved in the political process? The reason hell's legions have taken over is that the church has become silent. You need to go to the voting booth and vote your Judeo-Christian beliefs. And if a secular humanist is running against a man of God, vote for the man of God. If you vote for an abortionist, you're voting for murder to be the law of the land. If you vote for a homosexual, you're voting for sodomy, and you bring the judgment of God upon this nation. When you pull the lever, make it the right choice, because you, and your children, will live with it.

The second blessing in scripture is in Genesis 12, where God said to Abraham, "I will bless those that bless you and I will curse those that curse you." If you bless the nation of Israel and the Jewish people, God will bless you. If you oppress them, God will cut you off. It is a spiritual law that is indisputable.

The Jewish people have employed the principle of the blessing from that day until this. On the Sabbath, Jewish fathers and mothers bless their children in the name of the God of Abraham, Isaac and Jacob. When those children become 13, at something called a bar mitzvah for boys or a bat mitzvah for girls, the parents put their hands on them before the congregation and bless them in the name of Abraham, Isaac and Jacob. What are they saying and why are they doing it? They are literally shaping the destiny of those children. They are molding what they want those children to be in their future years.

Have you ever wondered why the Jewish people are so blessed? Why is it that the majority of Pulitzer Prize winners are Jewish people? Why are so many Jewish people successful in finance and commerce? May I suggest to you that it is found in the supernatural power of the blessing: The fathers bless their children and those children go right out and prosper because of the impartation of the blessing.

On the other hand, the Gentiles across the street are telling their kids, "You're stupid, you'll never amount to anything, you can't get anything right." On this side of the street the Goldbergs are telling their children, "Go out and conquer the world," and they're doing it. Now which do you want? Do you want to impart the blessing of God to your children, or do you want to poison their future by your words?

Then in Numbers 6, God gave to Moses the words that Aaron, the high priest, should speak to bless the people. "The Lord bless thee, and keep thee: the Lord make his face shine upon thee, and be gracious unto thee: the Lord lift up his countenance upon thee, and give thee peace" (Num. 6:24-26).

When Jesus began his public ministry, he began with the Sermon on the Mount. That sermon includes a series of nine blessings. It begins with, "Blessed are the poor in spirit" (Matt. 5:3). There are blessings on those who mourn, blessings on the meek and those who hunger and thirst after righteousness, blessings on the merciful and the pure in heart, blessings on the peacemakers and those who are persecuted for righteousness' sake. Nine powerful blessings that shape the destiny of the people that participate in them.

Once when Jesus was teaching, he stopped in the middle of his teaching to bless the children. The Bible says that "he took them up in his arms, put his hands upon them, and blessed them" (Mark 10:14). If Jesus blessed the children, why don't we? What did he say when he blessed them? I'll tell you what he said. He said what was in Numbers 6, and anything else that he desired to see come to pass in the life of that child.

The last thing Jesus did on this earth was to lift up his hands and pronounce a blessing as he departed into heaven. "And he led them out as far as to Bethany, and he lifted up his hands, and blessed them. And it came to pass, while he blessed them, he was parted from them, and carried up into heaven" (Luke 24:50-51).

The point is that imparting the blessing was his first and last priority. The first thing Jesus did in his ministry was to bless, and the last thing Jesus did on this earth was to bless. If he did it, why don't we do it? If he is our example, why don't we do it?

St. Paul understood the power and the purpose of the blessing. Every book he wrote begins with a divine blessing. He understood that in his spiritual authority as apostle he could speak a blessing upon the readers. Read any one of Paul's writings and it begins something like this," Grace and peace to you from God our Father and the Lord Jesus Christ." That's a blessing.

The blessing and spiritual warfare

Proverbs 26:2 says, "Like a fluttering sparrow or a darting swallow, an undeserved curse does not come to rest." Have you ever seen a swallow flying along and almost stop in mid-air and fly back the other way? This is what Solomon is referring to in this verse. He says that when a curse is coming at you like a darting swallow, if it is undeserved, it cannot find a place to rest and has to return to the sender.

Now follow this. The Bible says to bless those who persecute you. When you bless someone who curses you, it is not to demonstrate your goodness. It's not so you can say, "Well, I'm really holy. I am a special child of God, me and St. Paul. I should get me a cape with a big red A on it for apostle." That's not the message. It is to demonstrate that you're overcoming evil with good, because when I bless you in the name of the Lord, an invisible shield surrounds me. It is a prayer cover. And when you curse me, that curse cannot stick. If people curse me and I curse them back, then the root of bitterness gets in my heart and I'm separated from God. Then I have no joy and peace. But if someone curses me, or says something hateful to me, and I bless them in the name of the Lord, in that instant a shield comes around me and the curse without cause cannot come to rest. Like a darting swallow it returns to the sender.

The power and permanence of the blessing

Once the blessing is spoken into existence, it cannot be broken by men. It can be stopped by God because of disobedience, but not by man. The Bible illustration of that is found in Genesis 27. Isaac is old and his sight is failing him. Jacob, the "heel-catcher," comes in with his arms covered with lambskin, to deceive his father and get the blessing that should have gone to his older brother Esau. When Isaac put his hands on Jacob's arms, he says, "You feel like Esau, but you sound like Jacob." So Jacob seduced his father into giving him the blessing, and then left with it. No sooner had he left the tent than Esau came in and said, "Father, bless me." And Isaac said, "Who was it that I just blessed?" Esau realized his brother had deceived his father and he begged for a blessing. But Isaac said, "I have blessed Jacob and he will be blessed." The message is: I cannot rescind the blessing. Once it has been given, I cannot take it back. Isaac gave a blessing to Esau that was more of a curse than it was a blessing. He said, "You'll live by the sword and you will serve your younger brother."

Parents, when you speak, you begin to shape the destiny of your children. Here is further Bible evidence. When Jacob was about to die, he gathered his 12 sons around his bed. And he spoke into each of their lives a blessing. If you will follow the lives of those sons through scripture, every one of those sons lived out exactly what their father said.

When Jesus Christ was on earth, he had 12 disciples. He told them they were the light of the world and the salt of the earth. At that point in time, it was not true. They were filled with moral imperfection, still doubting who he was. One of them, Peter, who denied the Lord, attempted to kill one of the soldiers who came to arrest Jesus. So they were less than wonderful. But they did become the light of the world and the salt of the earth. The point is that they rose to the level of the prophecy. They literally became what he said because he shaped their destiny with the power of the blessing.

The power of the blessing at Calvary

In the Bible, the right hand symbolizes the greater blessing and the left hand symbolizes the lesser blessing. Jesus Christ is seated at the right hand of God the Father. That's the place of blessing. We have an expression, "he is my right-hand man." When Jacob blessed his grandchildren, he reversed his hands. The normal way would have been to bless the first-born with his right hand and second-born with his left hand. But when he brought his grandsons before him, he crossed his hands and gave the greater blessing to the second-born and the lesser blessing to the first-born. The boys' father, Joseph, saw what was happening and tried to stop him. But Jacob said, "Leave me alone. I know what I'm doing." (Well, that's a real loose translation. He took four or five verses to say it.) Jacob purposely gave the greater blessing to the second-born and the lesser blessing to the first-born.

This was a foreshadowing of the cross of Jesus Christ. Jesus Christ was the first-born of the father. He deserved the right hand of blessing. He deserved the best blessing, but he did not get it. On the cross he cried, "My God, My God, why hast thou forsaken me?" The father said, "I have not forsaken you. I have put my left hand upon you. But I have given the right hand of blessing today to the Gentile people, to the people who are no people, to the people who are outside the covenants of Abraham, to strangers who have no right to come before the throne of grace. Today I am giving them life everlasting and I'm placing upon you the hand of the death. I'm giving to them health and healing, but I'm giving to you the stripes on your back. I'm giving to them mercy, but I'm giving to you judgment. I'm giving to them acceptance, buy I'm giving to you rejection." And from that moment until this moment, every Gentile on the face of the earth has been privileged to say, "I am the seed of Abraham. I have the blessings of Abraham. All that God ever intended for his people, I can now have."

That is the purpose and the power of the blessing. When God gave Moses the blessing for the children of Israel he concluded by saying, "And they shall put my name upon the children of Israel; and I will bless them" (Numbers 6:27). When God places his name upon you, then you can expect the attributes of his name. In the Bible God allowed himself to be known by eight names that reveal his power, his purpose and his personality.

His name is **Jehovah Jireh**, which means "the Lord our provider." He will provide for all your needs — not your greeds, but your real needs. Paul said, "My God shall supply all your need according to his riches in glory by Christ Jesus" (Phil. 4:19). God will make a way where there seems to be no way. What God has done before, He will do again. He will not leave you alone; He will provide for you. His blessing is upon you through the authority of his name.

God provides where he guides. The place of his purpose is the place of his provision. Find God's purpose for your life, and you will find his provision. God provides what you cannot provide. Unlike the U. S. government, however, God expects you to work. For the past 30 years in America we have been destroying the traditional family through welfare. Here's how it works. If a 16-year-old girl gets angry with her parents and does not want to keep their rules and wants an apartment of her own, all she has do to is have an illegitimate baby. Then the government will give her a monthly check, free legal advice and free medical care. That's why illegitimacy in America has skyrocketed. If she wants a raise, all she has to do is have a second baby. Welfare is not God's plan for the family. It is time for the federal government to stop taking money from people who will work and giving it to people who won't work. And it is time for the federal government to stop tearing up the traditional family by subsidizing rebellion in the lives of teenagers.

His name is **Jehovah Nissi**, which means "the Lord our banner." The banner is a symbol of war, and the church of Jesus Christ is at war with the world, the flesh and the devil. America is engaged in warfare for its spiritual soul, and to the winner goes the prize of our children. I believe we have just a handful of years to turn this country around, so if you have something to do that will preserve America, do it now. This is the day for the church of Jesus Christ to stand up and to speak up for righteousness.

His name is **Jehovah Rohi**, which means "the Lord our shepherd." "The Lord is my Shepherd, I shall not want" (Ps. 23:1). I shall not want joy, because he anoints my head with oil. I shall not want forgiveness, because he restores my soul. I shall not want companionship, because he is a friend that sticketh closer than a brother. I shall not want prosperity, because he prepares a table before me in the presence of mine enemies. His goodness gives me the things that I do not deserve, and his mercy spares me from the things I do deserve.

He leads me beside still water. Why? Because sheep fear running water. Running water weights down the wool of a sheep and will drag it downstream and drown it. So when God leads you, he leads you to still water. It's what you need. It may not be what you want, but it's what you need.

He makes me to lie down in green pastures. Why? Because it is the responsibility of the sheep in the springtime to get fat. There were no Purina feed stores in those days, so the sheep had to get fat enough in the springtime to see them through the winter when grass was not available. The spiritual application is this. There will be seasons in your life when everything goes right. You're under the spout where the glory comes out and you just can't do anything wrong. You even go to the mall and there's a parking place right next to Joske's. Then winter comes, and nothing goes right. All the reserves that you have gathered are spent. It does not mean that God doesn't love you. It simply means you're going through a season, and soon it will be springtime. If you're going through a dark and disappointing moment, a depressing winter of your soul, I've got good news for you. The God that sent the winter will send the spring. It's hours away. If you'll rejoice and be exceedingly glad, God will restore all that you have lost and give it to you seven times over. And so shall he bless you.

His name is **Jehovah Rapha**, which means "the Lord our healer." I know there's a great controversy in the healing message. There are those who teach that Jesus never heals, and that's wrong. There are those who teach that Jesus heals every time, and that's wrong. But I believe that so long as you are living according to the purposes of God, Jesus Christ will heal you. God healed my mother of cancer. God healed my brother of epilepsy. He healed my uncle of a heart disease after my cousins, who were the doctors attending him, said to get the casket ready. But he's still living today, with the power and the blessing of God. Our God is a healing God, and he's still in the healing business.

His name is **Jehovah M'Kiddesh**, which means

"the Lord our holiness." The Bible says that without holiness, no man shall see the Lord. Most people aren't interested in hearing about holiness. But you won't get to heaven without it. You're not holy by what you do. You're holy because Christ makes you holy through his shed blood. Our faith is a holy faith. Our Bible is a holy Bible. Our God is the Holy God. Our city is the Holy City, the New Jerusalem. Our song recorded in the book of Revelation is "Holy, Holy, Holy, Lord God Almighty." I'm saying to you, church of Jesus Christ, it is time for us to be uniquely distinct from the world. The world is filled with greed and lust and materialism. It is time for the church to rise up, prepared to serve the Lord in the purity of holiness.

His name is **Jehovah Tsidkenu**, which means "the Lord our righteousness." Righteousness is living by the standard of God. The reason secular humanists hate the bible is that it gives an absolute definition of right and wrong, and they don't want anybody to tell them what's right and wrong. As long as everybody's opinion is equal, then God cannot dictate how you live. But when we stand before God Almighty on the day of judgment, we will not be judged by the Humanist Manifesto, we will be judged by the word of God. It is truth. Live by this word and know the power and the justice of Almighty God.

His name is **Jehovah Shalom**, which means "the Lord our peace." Shalom is a Jewish word that's all inclusive. It means hello, it means goodbye, it means may you be blessed in your family, may you be blessed in your health, your finances, and may peace be yours in all seasons. You cannot have the peace of God and be at war with God. Some of you are at war with God. You have chosen to disobey the word of God. You have made rebellion and anarchy the code of your life, and you will not have God's peace as long as you are in rebellion against spiritual authority. Our world longs for peace, but there will be no peace until Jesus Christ, the Prince of Peace, returns to earth.

Today in the name of Jesus, I bless you in the name of the Lord.

Chapter 11

Defeating Depression

We did a survey in our church to see what concerns the congregation most wanted to see addressed. Next to concerns about the marriage relationship, depression was something that a lot of people said they were facing. Depression can come over a number of things. Financial difficulties can trigger depression. You're knocking your brains out trying to make a living and every time you get both ends together, Congress moves the middle. Broken relationships and family crises can be a terrible burden. Unexplained tragedies and unexpected accidents occur. You face the loss of a loved one and suddenly what seemed so important yesterday is not even worth talking about today. Your life turns upside down and depression, like a tidal wave, sweeps over your soul.

When I'm talking about depression, please understand I'm not talking about clinical depression that needs medical attention. I'm talking about sadness, about the blues and the blahs. You feel gloomy and down in the dumps. You feel like the title of Erma Bombeck's book, *If Life Is Just A Bowl of Cherries, Why Am I Always in the Pits?*

Today I want you to hear from the word of God how to defeat depression. We're going to look at some people in the Bible who got depressed and what they did about it. I want you to leave this place today full of joy unspeakable and full of glory, rid of whatever in life is ripping you up and causing you grief.

Job lamented the fact that he didn't die the day he was born. "Why died I not from the womb? Why did I not give up the ghost when I came out of the belly?" (Job 3:11). You don't have to be Sigmund Freud to see depression in that. Unfortunately, some of you who have been raised with the theology that if you are Super Christian, you'll never be depressed. You'll somehow go through life without a trial and nothing will ever touch you. That's pure bunk and I want you to hear that first out. Everybody has problems. Great spiritual leaders in the word of God fought with this thing called depression, and they conquered it. You can, too.

Who gets depressed?

Almost everyone gets depressed sometime in their life. Moses received the ten commandments in a face to face encounter with God. When he came down from the mountain he found out that while he was gone his church elected a new pastor. Now that will depress you. While he was alone with God they had come up with a new theology, the golden calf theology. Israel wanted a god they could see and touch, just like the statues in your homes and on the dashboard of your car. When Moses returned to his flock on Sunday morning, he found them having sex orgies. Don't you know that would really depress a preacher? Moses threw down the ten commandments and crushed them to pieces. He said, "Just wait till you hear my new sermon series on Sin, Sex and Self-Control."

Elijah got depressed. Wicked old Jezebel sent Elijah a message and said, "I'm going to kill you by this time tomorrow." Elijah ran for his life out into the wilderness. He collapsed under a juniper tree and prayed, "Lord, go ahead and take my life. I'm the only one left that's living for you, and they're trying to kill me." Aren't you glad God doesn't answer every pity-pot prayer you pray? The Lord sent an angel to feed Elijah and strengthen him.

Charles Haddon Spurgeon, one of the greatest preachers of all time, nearly died from depression. One Sunday while he was preaching to a full congregation, a mentally handicapped man stood up and screamed, "Fire! Fire!" The huge crowd stampeded for the doors and four of Spurgeon's dear friends were trampled to death. His mind literally snapped. The deacons took him over to one of their homes and gave him the best medical counsel available. They prayed around the clock for the survival of their pastor. A few days later, while walking in the garden, Spurgeon said it was as if a light had pierced through the darkness and he could feel the presence of Jesus. "All that I had ever known was restored to me because of the counsel and the comfort of the dearest of friends," he said.

Smith Wigglesworth witnessed mighty miracles of God's power in his great healing crusades. Yet he would go home and roll on the floor in pain from kidney stones. He was depressed because God didn't heal him. He asked God why he healed all those other people but not him. Have you ever asked God why? God won't answer you. He doesn't have to explain it, he is the Lord. You have to receive what God does by faith. He is sovereign.

So everybody gets depressed from time to time, even super saints.

Eight major causes of depression

1. Extreme disappointment. No one ever gets depressed when everything is going right. When you've got money in the bank and everyone's healthy and your sports car is running well, who needs God? But when things go bad, when your business goes upside down or your marriage begins to fall apart, or you begin to have problems with your children, or your health fails, then, suddenly you need God. Don't be a crisis Christian. You need the Lord as a friend in all seasons. He's not something you run to every time that Blue Cross-Blue Shield can't come through.

2. Lack of self-esteem. The Bible says to love your neighbor as your self. The point is this, if you don't like yourself, you surely won't like your neighbor.

3. Unfair comparisons. There's not a verse in this Bible that says, "Compare yourselves one with the other." Comparing yourself with someone else is unscriptural, ungodly and will always lead to depression. There will always be somebody in your profession better than you. There will always be a better doctor, a better lawyer, a better salesman. Be all you can be and forget it. There will always be somebody prettier than you or more handsome than you. Be all you can be and then forget it. Your genetic code determines what you're going to look like and that was determined the instant there was a conception in your mother's body. If you had good looking parents, you will be good looking, thus saith the Lord. But if you didn't, you get to look like the rest of us.

4. Sense of being trapped. When you feel trapped in an intolerable situation — a bad marriage, a shaky business deal, a church crisis, a major illness — you will battle depression.

5. Unrealistic goals. You can be anything in life you want to be, but you can't be everything. You can be a brain surgeon, or you can be a boxer, or you can be an author, but you can't be all three of those at the same time. When you have unrealistic goals, you will constantly be frustrated. Do not try to do something God hasn't equipped you to do.

6. Biological malfunction. A woman came to my office and said, "I have a demon. I want you to cast it out." I said, "Before I start living by your prognosis, let's talk." We talked a while and I said, "There's nothing about you that speaks of demon possession. You need to go to the doctor and get a good physical examination." (Don't you good super-faith people turn the television off right here, because there are times that good people do need medical doctors. Someday even you might need one.) She did go to the doctor and after he balanced out her hormones, she was singing like a lark. She thought I was a genius. Not so. It is plainly dumb not to take care of your physical body. You only have one. Don't destroy your physical body by trying to make it do what God didn't equip it to do. If you make it live on junk food and make it live unreasonable hours, it will break down — and you can't just go down to Sears and get some spare parts. So treat your physical body well because it is the temple of the Holy Spirit.

7. Postpartum depression. Shortly after the birth of her child, the bubbly, bright, breezy mother sinks into the blues and the blahs. She cries about everything. She feels she's going to hurt her baby. She thinks she's not a good mother. That's not true. It's just an emotional response to what her body has gone through.

8. Hyperactivity. A super achiever gets to be 50 or 60 and your mind can still go 120 but your body can only go 40. And you react in frustration, refusing to slow down. You sink into depression thinking you're a failure. Face it superman, you've reached the age of baldness, bifocals and bunions. It's a wonderful time in life; it's called reality.

Who stays depressed

Who stays depressed? Those who choose to.

Some of you are majoring in your problem. All you want to do is wade through the sewer of yesterday, remembering what happened to you back in 1942, or 1962, or 1982. I'm telling you in the name of Jesus Christ, forget it. "Forgetting those things which are behind," Paul said (Phil. 3:13). Think on things that are good and wholesome, that are honest and true — and when you possess those thoughts, you will have a hope that is steadfast and sure. You won't be thinking about your problems, you'll be rejoicing in the solutions that Jesus Christ has given you on the authority of God's word.

The Bible says, "Hope thou in God" (Ps. 42:5). "Have not I commanded thee? Be strong and of a good courage; be not afraid, neither be thou dismayed" (Joshua 1:9). "Rejoice in the Lord always; and again I say, rejoice," Paul wrote (Phil. 4:4). You rejoice by choice. It's something you decide to do. You must be willing to face the fact that your mental attitude toward the circumstance, not the circumstance itself, is the cause of your unhappiness. Until you're willing to admit that, you're incurable. Even God can't help you.

How people try to escape from depression

When you injure an arm, you automatically withdraw it, trying to keep other people from touching it. You do the same thing emotionally. When you're hurt emotionally, you withdraw and try to insulate yourself, to keep other people from hurting you. Eventually you withdraw from reality. Years ago when there was plenty of property and you got in a feud with somebody, you could go over the hill and start Hageeville. But it wasn't long before we spread from sea to shining sea. And now the world is a community. We cannot escape each other; we have to learn how to live with each other. Rich, poor, educated, uneducated, white, black, brown, Jew, Christian, Moslem — we have to learn to live with each other under the canopy of heaven.

Alcoholics are trying to get in the bottle and escape the real world. You can't do it. There is no answer in alcohol. You won't find happiness in a bottle. And you won't find it smoking crack or sniffing white powder. Some Christians live on Valium. That is not the New Testament life-style. If you have to take a pill, take the "gos-pill." It will give you the answers to life.

Some people try to escape depression by eating too much. Sometimes when people get depressed or stressed out, they try to eat everything that's in the refrigerator — every night. You know, when you get saved and you give up "the world," you give up drinking, you give up drugs, all you can do is eat. The difference between a

Pentecostal and an Episcopalian is that a Pentecostal will go home from church and eat everything in the house, and then criticize the Episcopalian for getting drunk. Gluttony and drunkenness are equally bad.

Exhibitionism is a way of trying to escape depression. A child will begin to have temper tantrums. I had two or three of those as a child. I lost my temper, and my dad helped me find it. Women will talk too much. Men will gamble obsessively. Teenage boys will drive recklessly or steal a car for a joyride. A teenage girl will become promiscuous. Suicide is a form of exhibitionism, an attempt to grab attention from family and friends.

Clinging is a manifestation of people who are trying to escape depression. A child will cling to parents who don't have enough time for him or her. When a child grows up in a home where the parents do not show affection or approval, that child grows up to be an insecure adult and continues to cling and grasp for love. Adult clinging manifests itself in excessive generosity, paying for things that are far beyond your means because you are trying to buy someone's love. If the people you know won't love you for who you are, quit trying to buy their affection. It's not worth it. Insecure women may become compulsive hostesses who go overboard wining and dining guests so that people will always like them. That's insecurity, not generosity.

Another manifestation of clinging is making oneself indispensable. Insecure men will work long hours at the office, more than anyone else, trying to prove they're indispensable to the company. You know what? The cemetery is filled with indispensable men. When you die the sun will still rise and set, the grass will continue to grow and nothing will change. So go home and introduce yourself to your wife and children and say, "Hi, kids, I'm

Dad. I'm the reason you're here." I've never seen a man on his deathbed ask to see the watch they gave him for 25 years of loyal service down at the insurance company. But I have heard them talk about the good times they had together and the special times they sacrificed for each other. So go home and give your family the best gift you can give anybody — yourself!

Physical symptoms of depression

1. Erratic sleep patterns. Some people sleep too much when they're depressed, trying to escape their sadness. Other people can't sleep at all when they're depressed. Matthew 11:28 says, "Come unto me, all ye that labor and are heavy laden, and I will give you rest." If you're living like hell, however, you can't have the peace of God. If you're smoking dope, you're going to be depressed. You can't break the laws of righteousness and have the peace of God. You can't have the peace of God and be at war with God.

2. Apathy. You have the blahs; things just don't interest you any more. You feel tired all the time. You're unmotivated about anything.

3. Loss of appetite.

4. Loss of sex drive.

5. Unkempt appearance. How you dress is a direct reflection of how you feel about yourself. A sloppy dresser is a man or a woman who has given up on himself or herself. I read a book by a concentration camp survivor who said that in the hell of the holocaust she could tell when people were getting ready to die, because they quit taking care of themselves. She said, "I tied my shoestrings even though they were rotten, and I combed my hair with whatever I could find, because I didn't want the Nazis ever to believe that I had given up on myself."

Emotional symptoms of depression

1. Loss of affection. When a person stops giving love, he has the worst kind of sickness in the world. It is better to give love and to be hurt than not to give it at all. Jesus commanded us to love one another; he said that's how the world would know that we're his disciples. When you refuse to give love, you die. The spiritual principle is this: Unless you love other people and love yourself, you will literally kill yourself.

2. Sadness. To live in a joyless state is an unhealthy, ungodly way to live. It shows on your face. As depression increases you lose all ability to respond to humor and often resent those who are joyful. You have a face that looks like a Missouri mule. You are the kind of people who make drunks glad they're drunks. You are a walking billboard for the misery of the kingdom of God. What you need to do is get saved and filled with the Holy Spirit, because the fruit of the spirit is love, joy and peace.

3. Weeping. Depressed people often have an involuntary tendency to cry. They think nobody cares, but Psalm 34:17 says, "The righteous cry, and the Lord heareth."

4. Hostility. Do you get angry with your wife and children for no reason at all? "Whoever is angry with his brother without a cause shall be in danger of the judgment" (Matt. 5:22), which describes many people who go to the house of God. If you're a child abuser or wife abuser, I pray the next time you reach out your hand to hit, that God will wither your arm from the elbow out. If that doesn't happen, I hope your wife picks up a skillet and parks it right between your eyes.

5. *Anxiety, fear, worry.*

6. *Hopelessness.* Hopelessness comes when you reject the hope of God. Romans 15:13 says, "Now the God of hope fill you with all joy and peace in believing, that ye may abound in hope, through the power of the Holy Ghost." "Go thy way, eat thy bread with joy, and drink thy wine with a merry heart" (Ecc. 9:7). John 15:11 says, "These things have I spoken unto you ... that your joy might be full." Jesus was happy. He gave us three cheers: Be of good cheer, I have overcome the world. Be of good cheer, thy sins be forgiven thee. Be of good cheer, it is I; be not afraid.

Seven steps to defeating depression

1. *Attack your problem with the word of God.* I believe in counseling, but I don't believe in eternal counseling. I believe you should go to look for a solution, not to look for a routine for the rest of your life. I believe at the root of most problems is sin — and when you're ready to stop the sin, you'll find the peace of God. When you start living by the word of God, lots of things solve themselves instantly. A Christian chooses to be depressed when he refuses to live by the principles of God's word. Living by God's principles produces love, joy and peace. Whoever does not have the fruit of the spirit is not living in the spirit. Quit chattering about being spirit-filled when you're walking around acting like you were baptized in lemon juice. If you've accepted Christ, you're

a new creature.

2. *Spend some time every day meditating on the word of God.* Your mind is like a computer, and as they say in the computer business: garbage in, garbage out. When you read Playboy, that's garbage in, and all that can come out is garbage. When all you think about is trash, all that can come out is trash. If you want to have the happiness of God, have the holiness of God. "Blessed is the man ... [whose] delight is in the law of the Lord; and in his law doth he meditate day and night" (Psalm 1:2). When you meditate on the word of God day and night, when you think about things that are good, true, honest, and of good report, your brain will be affected with the hope that is steadfast and sure.

3. *Get rid of grudges every day.* Ephesians 4:26 says if you're angry, don't sin by nursing a grudge. "Don't let the sun go down on your wrath." Get over it quickly, for when you are angry, you give foothold to the devil. Do you have a temper problem? Get it solved before the day is over, or else you'll kill yourself.

4. *Spend some time every day getting to be more intimate* with your husband or wife, your children, your parents, your brothers or sisters, because family harmony is essential to your mental and spiritual health. Unresolved family conflicts will destroy you.

5. *Spend some time each week with committed Christians* who are full of the spirit. Proverbs 13:20 says, "He that walketh with wise men shall be wise: but a companion of fools will be destroyed." Get with people of like precious faith and fellowship with them. When you run with a group of lounge lizards, you'll be a lounge lizard. When you associate with crooks, you'll be a crook. You want to be depressed? Go in business with a crook. You don't have friends? The Bible says that if you want

friends, you must show yourself friendly (Prov. 18:24).

6. Go to work on something that brings personal satisfaction to you. The three faces of happiness are something to do, something to love, and something to hope for.

7. Do something nice for one special person every week. "Give and it shall be given unto you," Luke 6:38 says. What do you want other people to give to you? Then give that to them. It can be your time, it can be your love, it can be flowers, it can be a card, it can be a bowl of red beans, but give something special on a regular basis. You'll find that by giving your life away, you'll find it.

Chapter 12

You Can't Go Home Again

Years ago Thomas Wolfe wrote a novel called *You Can't Go Home Again.* It was about the people in his home town, Asheville, North Carolina. After achieving success as a writer, Wolfe returned to his home town. He found it was not the same town. It had changed and the people had changed. So he wrote the book *You Can't Go Home Again.* Wolfe rattled every skeleton in every closet in Asheville, and the people in that city hated him for it.

The theme of Wolfe's book is this: you can never go back and pick up the threads of a life that used to be. No matter how homesick you may be for it, no matter how nostalgic you may feel about it, no matter how romantically inclined you are toward the past, you can't go back. It's gone, and gone forever.

It was Plato who said that you can never look at the same river twice. If you look at the river once and look away, when you look back, the river you saw a moment ago is already gone. And so it is with life. You cannot live life looking over your shoulder. Life is made to live in the now. You can't go home again. You can't go back to the romantic past. You can't go back to something that used to be.

That's why we hate change. Our lives in the 20th century are changing so rapidly. Your own body is changing. In your youth you ran a 100-yard dash and they timed you with a stopwatch. Now they use an hourglass, or a calendar. You don't think you're changing? Go home and try to put on the military uniform you mustered out in 25 years ago when you had a 30" waist. Now your clothes are made by Omar the Tentmaker. You have knees that buckle and pants that won't.

Your family is constantly changing. Mother, when you took your six-year-old out to catch the school bus the very first time, you did it with a lump in your throat. You were living a day that could never be repeated. Your baby comes home in a few hours changed, more mature than he's ever been. He's been to school. The tricycle will be replaced with a bicycle. Pretty soon that bicycle will be replaced with a Buick. One day they're babies and before you know it they've become teenagers. Their hormones go berserk, their brains go AWOL, and a phone starts growing out their ear. The next thing you know, they'll drag some fuzzy-faced cretin into your living room and say, "I want to marry this protoplasmic non-entity." You control your urge to upchuck because you know that once they're married, they can never come home again. On, they'll come back to visit, but it will never be quite the same. So many changes.

I choose this message today because there are many of you who are living your life romantically remembering a past that is gone forever. America is presently romantically remembering the 1950s. It was a time of tranquility and security. We "liked Ike." Everything was wholesome. Now in the 1990s we have abortion, AIDS, mass murder, homosexuality, pornography, Satanism. It is no wonder we are clutching for the security of the past. But you cannot go back to the past; it's over and done with. You can't go home again.

Many of you are looking at a grand and glorious moment in your past and you're trying to live in the glow of that glory. You can't. It's gone forever. You can't go home again. For some of you the past was not grand and glorious, but bitter and painful. You're looking back at a marriage that failed, buried in guilt and remorse. You tried your best, but the love of your life is gone, for whatever reason, and your heart is crushed. You can't go back to that. Some of you are mired in sorrow and heartache, looking back at the yawning mouth of a tiny grave where your precious baby was laid. You can't go back to that. All the tears you can shed won't change that. Some of you are remembering a business failure that destroyed your dreams. Some of you are remembering a bad decision you made that critically altered your life. It's in the past and you need to forget it.

If the past was bitter, forget it. If the past was beautiful, forget it. Paul said, "Forgetting those things which are behind, and reaching forth unto those things which are before, I press toward the mark for the prize of the high calling of God in Christ Jesus" (Phil. 3:13-14). Forget the good and forget the bad, because you can't go home again.

The example I give to demonstrate that you can't go home again is the story of the children of Israel and their exodus from Egypt. It is a classic study of human nature and how people respond to change. Listen very closely and you will find yourself in this sermon.

> *That night all the people of the community raised their voices and wept aloud. All the Israelites grumbled against Moses and Aaron, and the whole assembly said to them, "If only we had died in Egypt! Or in this desert! Why is the Lord bringing us to this land only to let us fall by the sword? Our wives and children will be taken as plunder. Wouldn't it be better for us to go back to Egypt?" And they said to each other, "We should choose a leader and go back to Egypt."* (Numbers 14:1-4)

The Exodus is a classic story of how people respond to change. The children of Israel were slaves in Egypt. They had been beaten with whips like animals. They had been abused, starved and worked beyond endurance. They were living in shacks, dressed in rags. The Egyptians had taken their male babies and drowned them in the Nile river. Do you see a need for change here? The children of Israel prayed one prayer for 400 years. "Lord God of Abraham, Isaac and Jacob, send us a deliverer. Set us free from Pharaoh." There was a great need for change, and a great desire for a change. But with change comes challenge. There are five challenges they had to face in order to leave Egypt and make it to the promised land. And if you do not overcome these five challenges, you will never break out of the bondage of your past.

It looks impossible

When you've been beaten and oppressed for 400 years, it's easy to think that change is impossible. When justice has been denied or delayed for years, when you've made bricks for Pharaoh every day of your life, just like your father and your grandfather and your great grandfather, when you work in a mud hole up to your waist, it's pretty easy to say, "This is normal life. This is just the way things are." It gets pretty easy to look across the breakfast table at your wife and say, "Mary, the ghetto is as good as it gets. Our God supplies no better than this. Our '52 Chevy with the tail pipe tied to the back bumper with baling wire is as good as it gets."

Go back with me in the theater of your mind and see two men who are on their way to work to make bricks for Pharaoh. They're talking as they're on their way to the mud hole. Howard says to Herman, "Look, we've been talking about this promise of God delivering us from Pharaoh's bondage. But do you see any way God could possibly get us out of here? I mean, we've been here for 400 years. Pharaoh has the mightiest army on the face of the earth." Herman says, "Yeah, I know. It looks impossible." Howard agrees. "How are we going to be fed? There are at least two million of us. That would take millions of pounds of food a day. How are we going to be able to do that out in the wilderness? It's impossible. And where are we going to get water for two million people and our cows. It's impossible. And what about medical provision? We'll get out there and die, Herman. You know it's 120° in the day and at night it's freezing. How are we going to ever be able to survive out there? Then there's this guy Moses running around with a crooked stick that turns into a snake. What do you think about that, Herman?" Herman says, "Look, I quit going to church a long time ago. I gave up on miracles. Get in this mud hole, Goldberg, and let's make bricks till we die. This faith stuff is just impossible. We're going to be here until we're bleached bones like our grandfathers.

We might as well give up and get used to it."

Some of you have that mentality. You've thought, "There's no way God can get me out of this mess. I know God created the heavens in seven days, he spared the family of Noah in the flood, and he held the sun still for Joshua. But he can't help me, bless God. Poor, pitiful me."

Saints of God, nothing is impossible with our God. "But you don't know about my situation, preacher." I don't care about your situation. Have you been praying about it 400 years? They had. Nothing is impossible in your job situation. Nothing is impossible in your marriage. Nothing is impossible in your messed up finances, your health, your addictive habits. Nothing is impossible with God. You may have walked in here today with no reason to live, with every dream in your life shattered and crushed. But you can walk out of here today free from all sin, free from all iniquity, free from every addictive habit — free because Jesus Christ has made us free. Quit wading around in the bone yard of your past, griping and grumbling about how pitiful life is. Start rejoicing in your salvation and recognize that you are a child of king.

"But I've been praying for soooooooo long." God's delays are not God's denials. So what if Pharaoh has the mightiest army on earth. God Almighty can drown him in three feet of water. You need two million people fed in the wilderness? God will rain Mrs. Baird's bread from heaven every morning. Their clothes did not wear out for 40 years. No one got sick for 40 years. I don't know what kind of health care program Bill Clinton's going to come up with, but I guarantee it won't match what God gave the children of Israel in the wilderness. The cloud by day blocked the sun, the fire by night raised the temperature to 72°. Moses hit a rock and out came enough water to refresh all the people and their livestock. God can supply. Nothing is impossible with our God.

Some of you have been spiritually and emotionally browbeaten. You have been humiliated, dehumanized, and emotionally whipped. You are tired and exhausted. Quitting looks good and victory seems impossible. But Egypt is not your inheritance, the promised land is. Forget what is behind and press on to what God has for you. Your inheritance is not sin and sickness. Your inheritance is divine health and healing. Your inheritance is not financial crisis, your inheritance is having God supply all your needs (not your greeds, but your needs). Your heritage is not to live in a domestic squabble that's a perpetual civil war. It is for the husband to love his wife as Christ loved the church and for the wife to submit herself to her husband. That's the teaching of the New Testament. Your spiritual heritage is not to be in bondage to drugs and alcohol. Your heritage is to be free, for whom the Son sets free is free indeed. You need to walk out of this church today and kick the mud of Pharaoh's brick pits off your feet and say, "I'm a child of the king. I'm not destined to live in bondage in Egypt. I'm destined to live in the promised land of milk and the honey, and nothing is impossible with God."

You have to get out of Egypt to get to the promised land. It took God one or two days to get the Jews out of Egypt, but it took 40 years to get Egypt out of them. You have to give up what you have to get what God has for you. You have to give up what you consider good for what God says is better. Why is it that when God gives us something, we roll it up and hold on to it like a bulldog biting the last bone in the world? We say, "I'll never give this up." God says, "I have something better for you," but you don't believe it. If God is trying to take something away from you, let him. Because what he replaces it with will be milk and honey, not the mud pits of Egypt.

The children of Israel could have been content to live in the past but for the barrier of the Red Sea. Our text, Numbers 4, says they got together and decided to go back to Egypt. Do you know why they didn't? Not because they were spiritual, not because they were thankful for what God did for them, but because God closed the Red Sea again. They would have drowned trying to get back. As they approached the Red Sea, Pharaoh's army is behind them. To the south is the desert. To the north are the mountains. Immediately in front of them is Sea World, a wet and wild water experience. Has God ever started to do new things in your life and he brought you to the bank of the Red Sea? And you said, "This is impossible. No way is God going to be able to get all of us from here to there before that man's army devours all of us." That's what the children of Israel thought.

Never reject a new idea because it seems impossible. Never reject a new idea because it wasn't yours. God may have something new and wonderful to get you out of that rut you're in. A rut is nothing but a grave with both ends kicked out of it. It is better to do something imperfectly than to do nothing flawlessly. You cannot win if you don't begin.

It looked impossible when the three Hebrew children were thrown into the fiery furnace. The fire was so hot that the men who threw them in were cooked. But when they hit bottom there was a fourth man with them, one who looked like the son of God. They walked out of the fire without the smell of smoke and not a hair on their head singed. It seemed impossible, but it happened.

When Daniel was thrown into the lion's den, it looked impossible. Those lions had been starved so they would attack Daniel with a fierceness that would thrill his captors. But the hands of the angels bound the mouths of the lions and Daniel slept that night on a fur-lined couch while the king walked in his bed chamber drinking Maalox, worrying about the man of God. Nothing is impossible with God.

It seemed impossible when the angel Gabriel went to a teenager by the name of Mary and said, "You're going to be the mother of the savior of the world." She said, "How shall this be, seeing I know not a man?" The angel said the Holy Spirit would come upon her, and then out of her soul gushed the words, "Be it unto me according to your word. For with God nothing shall be impossible." She could have said, "Look, I just can't do it. Those women down at my church will never have enough faith to believe my situation. If you think I'm going to ruin my schoolgirl figure to have that baby, there's no chance." She did not. She immediately submitted to the plan of the father. Nothing is impossible with God.

Longing for the good old days

The second challenge is to quit longing for the "good old days" and forget the past. If the past was great, forget it. If it was bad, forget it. You can't go home again. The past is gone forever. You only have today. So live your life holding the hand of God, following the cloud by day and the fire by night toward the destiny God has for you.

Look at Israel. Two million slaves walked out of downtown Cairo singing *Don't Fence Me In.* God took them across the Red Sea and drowned Pharaoh and his army. They passed out the tambourines and had a charismatic dance. Some 75,000 to 100,000 women followed Miriam as they began to praise the Lord for the great victory he had given them. But just 72 short hours later, following the cloud by day and the fire by night, they came to Marah, the place of bitter waters. And they ran straight to Pastor Moses and said, "Why did you bring us out here? We should have stayed in Egypt." How quickly we forget the great blessings of God. In Egypt they were being starved, they were being beaten, their children were being drowned. Moses leads them out of bondage, with God's miraculous help, and three days later it's his fault this happened.

It's no different today. There's a teaching in the charismatic community that goes like this: If you're really living a spiritual life, you'll never have a problem. That's heresy. It was God who took them from the Red Sea to the bitter water. How do I know God took them? Because the cloud by day and the fire by night were controlled by God. They had no choice but to follow that cloud, no choice but to stay under that fire by night. Why did God lead them to the bitter waters? God had to let them see what was in them before they could be what God wanted them to be. Many of us want God to do something for us. But God has to do something *in* us and *through* us before he can do something *for* us.

When God brings you to the bitter waters, don't throw up your hands and say, "God, why did you let this happen to me?" Just say, "Lord, I do not understand why you're doing what you're doing. But I trust that what you're about to give me is greater than anything I ever had in Egypt. I trust in your sovereign grace and your infinite love and I receive your blessing today, because I know you're the God that delivers."

"Why did you bring us out?" they asked Moses. Has God ever taken your well-ordered, predictable, business-as-usual, boring life and turned it upside down? Did you roll out your lower lip and scream, "Why didn't I stay in Egypt?" The words will be different, but the thought is the same. "Why did I ever buy this new house?" God leans over the balcony of heaven and says, "Because you got on your face and bawled and squalled for it, Bubba, and I gave it to you. Forget that the foundation is cracked, the roof leaks, the commode won't flush and the doors won't shut. You asked for it." Welcome to the promised land. "Why did I ever get married?" Because you told God that if you could have Leroy, you'd be happy for the rest of your life. Well, you've got Leroy. Rejoice, he's your choice!

The children of Israel did not go back to Egypt because God closed the Red Sea and forbade them to go back. You can't go home again. Quit longing for the "good old days." You can't go back to the past, no matter how bitter or blessed, so forget it and press on to the destiny God has for you.

It's not logical

The third challenge is the battle for the mind: carnal reasoning versus spiritual revelation. It's about doing things God's way as opposed to man's way.

The logical way to the promised land was a 14-day hike straight through the wilderness. Logic says that's the way to go. But God purposely took them the long way around. Exodus 13:17 says, "When Pharaoh let the people go, God did not lead them on the road through the Philistine country, though that was shorter. For God said, 'If they face war, they might change their minds and return to Egypt.'"

The Bible says there is a war between your mind, the carnal mind, and God's mind. Romans 8:7 says "the carnal mind is enmity against God." Romans 12:2 says, "Be not conformed to this world: but be ye transformed by the renewing of your mind." Philippians 2:5 says, "Let this mind be in you, which was also in Christ Jesus." The Bible says to serve the Lord with all of your heart, soul, mind and body.

God is waging a war for his church through his word. Satan is waging a war for his people through the television. You can watch it and see one violent, demonic thing after the other. Some of you are letting your children be reared by the television. The television is your baby sitter. It is your entertainment, and it is filled with things that are contrary to the nature and goodness of God. On the other hand there is the Bible, which God is trying to get his church to read. Let me ask you this: If you watch television 48 hours a week and read God's word five minutes a week, who's ruling your family, the Holy Spirit or Hollywood? That's an honest question.

There's a war going on for your mind. The Lord knows the best way. But if you let someone else lead you, they'll lead you into a deep ditch and you'll die in the wilderness and be nothing but bleached bones, outside the promises of God. You say, "Preacher, it doesn't make any sense the way God is leading." Hear this important word. You do not have to understand in order to obey God. God's way does not have to sound logical to you.

Telling Elijah to pour 12 barrels of water on a sacrifice when he was going to burn it up with fire was not logical. It did not make sense, but Elijah did it. I'm sure Elijah told God, "I don't know how you people start fires up there in heaven, but we don't pour water on things we want to burn up." God says, "I don't care if it's not logical, just do it." Elijah did, and fire fell from heaven and consumed the sacrifice.

Telling Peter to go fishing to get the money to pay his taxes was not logical. Jesus said, "Peter, I want you to get in the boat this morning and go catch a fish. There will be enough money in its mouth to pay our IRS bill." Doesn't that sound a little wacky to you? Peter could have said, "Look, I'm a professional fisherman and you're an unemployed carpenter. Who are you to tell me how to fish?" But he did, and the first fish he caught had the money in its mouth.

What's logical about a person walking into this church full of sin, their life in ruins, and they walk the aisle and ask God to save them and then walk out of this church forgiven of all their sins and totally free? There's nothing logical about it, but it happens every day we open the doors of this church, thank God.

What's logical about tithing? What's logical about giving 10% of your income to God and expecting to prosper more than people who don't? There's nothing logical about it. You won't find it in the Wall Street Journal, but I can assure you on the authority of God's word, that if you give God 10% of your income, you'll prosper more on the 90% than your neighbor will on the 100% he's stolen from God. Try tithing, it works.

Holding on to the familiar

God provided bread from heaven for the Israelites in the wilderness. Every day, without fail, enough to feed them all. But they longed for the old familiar things of Egypt. "We remember the fish we ate in Egypt at no cost — also the cucumbers, melons, leeks, onions and garlic ... and huevos rancheros and jalapeños. Now all we have out here in this wilderness is manna and we're tired of it." I'm sure Mrs. Moses had published a best seller called *101 Ways to Serve Manna*. But still they complained about God's provision. They said, "We want meat!" Numbers 11 says the Lord became "exceedingly angry" with them. God said, "You want meat? I'll give you meat." Then he caused the wind to bring quail from the ends of the earth, so many quail they could knock them down with their hands. All you could see, for a day's walk in any direction, was quail. The Bible says that while the meat was still in their mouth, the Lord's anger was kindled against them and he struck them with a plague (verse 33). You know, when God's providing for you, you ought to be real careful before you start criticizing the cooking.

The point is that when God says, "This is the way, walk ye in it," don't look back over your shoulder at Egypt. You can't go home again.

Wrestling with giants

The ultimate test, the last and the greatest test, the test that comes just before the victory, is the giants in the land.

The Israelites are at the Jordan River. Joshua and Caleb are coming back from Canaan to report on the possibilities and the potential that God has for them in the promised land. They are carrying a cluster of luscious grapes so large they have to use a pole to bring it. Winn Dixie doesn't have grapes that big. The children of Israel said, "Where did you get those grapes?" Joshua grinned and said, "Right next door to the biggest giant you've ever seen." Can't you hear them? "Giants? Did you say giants? You mean, after all we've been through — after the Red Sea experience, after the earthquake for worshipping the golden calf, after the snakes came out to bite us for murmuring, after the plague for criticizing God's cooking, after circling around in the wilderness for 40 years — now you're telling us that if we get the grapes we have to whip the giants?" Joshua said, "That's about it."

In the book of Ephesians the church of Jesus Christ is presented as seven things. The sixth thing they are is the bride of Christ. The seventh thing they are is the army of God. The last form of the church on earth is as an army, advancing and conquering. Some of you had rather be lovers than fighters. You'd rather be the bride than be in the army. But if you're going to have God's blessing between here and the rapture, you'd better put on the whole armor of God — because it's going to be a knuckle-busting fist fight between here and the gates of glory. Give Satan no ground. We are the blood-bought church of Jesus Christ, the army of the Living God, and the victory is ours in Jesus' name.

So when the giant marches up on your territory, or invades your home, kick that giant in the shins and say, "Back up, buzzard breath. I've been walking across this wilderness for 40 years. I haven't had a shower since Harry Truman was president. I've got grit in my hair and grit in my teeth. I've had no opportunity to sit down and rest and I'm in no mood for *Let's Make A Deal.* I want to be free from you — so get out of my life, in Jesus' name."

I want to challenge you today. I'm looking at some wonderful people who are hypnotized by the familiar, lulled by the sacredness of sameness. I want you to be all that God wants you to be. Risk reaching for a new horizon. Be free from the familiar of Egypt. Discover the excitement of following Jesus one step at a time until you reach the promised land flowing with milk and honey. You will hear voices calling out to you to come back to the same old rut where it's comfortable. But there's a voice within you that says, "Nothing is impossible with God." Reach out for all that God has for you. And regardless of how good the past was, or how bad it was, forget it. You can't live your life looking over your shoulder. You can't go home again.

Twelve Sunday Mornings with Pastor John Hagee
Volume 2

The sermons in this book are available on audio and VHS video cassettes. Hear these messages exactly as Pastor Hagee preached them for the congregation of Cornerstone Church in San Antonio, Texas, and television viewers across the nation.

S228A	Seven Secrets of Success *7 audio tapes*	$42
S228V	Seven Secrets of Success *7 video tapes*	$140
	(Canadian price: $56 audio, $175 video)	
S303A	Blessing or Curses *3 audio tapes*	$18
S303V	Blessing or Curses *3 video tapes*	$60
	(Canadian price: $24 audio, $75 video)	
206A	Defeating Depression *audio tape*	$6
206V	Defeating Depression *video tape*	$20
245A	You Can't Go Home Again *audio tape*	$6
245V	You Can't Go Home Again *video tape*	$20
	(Canadian price: $8 audio, $25 video)	

To order, send check or money order to the address below. Or order by telephone and charge your order to your MasterCard, VISA or Discover Card.

**John Hagee Ministries
PO Box 1400
San Antonio, TX 78295-1400
(210) 491-5100**

Call between 7:00 am. and midnight CST
7 days a week